# My First Ladies

*Twenty-five Years as the White House Chief Floral Designer*

*Behind the Scenes with First Ladies* MICHELLE OBAMA,
LAURA BUSH, HILLARY CLINTON, BARBARA BUSH,
NANCY REAGAN, *and* ROSALYNN CARTER

NANCY CLARKE
*with* CHRISTIE MATHESON

SELLERS
PUBLISHING

Published by Sellers Publishing, Inc.

Copyright © 2011 Nancy Clarke
All rights reserved.

Sellers Publishing, Inc.
161 John Roberts Road, South Portland, Maine 04106
Visit our Web site: www.sellerspublishing.com • E-mail: rsp@rsvp.com

ISBN 13: 978-1-4162-0639-2
Library of Congress Control Number: 2011921888

10 9 8 7 6 5 4 3 2 1

Printed in China.

# Dedication

*To Rosalynn Carter, Nancy Reagan, Barbara Bush, Hillary Clinton,
Laura Bush, and Michelle Obama, who each shared a small part
of their lives with me while they served our country as wonderful first ladies.*

*To the Residence staff of the White House, unsung heroes whose mission
is to make a home for the president and his family, and to keep the
White House in its glory.*

*And to my family, whose love and understanding made it possible for me to
work at the White House for thirty years.*

# Contents

# PREFACE: Blossoming Passion

I have loved flowers since the first day I saw my grandfather's garden. When I was growing up in Illinois, we didn't have much money, and we had to occupy ourselves with activities that didn't cost anything, like playing in our grandparents' yard. This was one of my favorite things to do. My grandfather was a professional gardener who maintained estate gardens, and he made his own yard beautiful, too, filling it with many colors and varieties of flowers.

We lived with my grandparents for a few years, and then moved half a block away, so I spent a lot of time in that yard — sometimes just looking at the blossoms, but more often picking the flower heads off the stems and squeezing snow berries to make them pop. "Nancy! Get out of those flower beds!" was my grandfather's constant refrain. When that didn't work, he tried to explain ("Don't pick the flowers off the stems, because they need to finish growing") or bargain with me ("You can water the flowers — if you stay out of the flower beds"). I loved watering the flowers, but I didn't stay out of his flower beds, which meant I would be temporarily banished from the yard. And then I'd sneak into other people's yards to play with their flowers, which always prompted a phone call to my mother. Eventually, I learned to stop destroying the flowers and to start caring for them almost as lovingly as my grandfather did.

My grandmother loved their flowers, but she wasn't as worried about my exploits in the garden. She was a seamstress who could sew the most exquisite things, from winter coats to wedding gowns, and she instilled in me a love of creativity. I think I got some of my artistic sensibilities from her. (When I was in grade school, I used to win a lot of little art contests — and I like to think that many of the flower arrangements I made for the White House were temporary works of art, too!)

I didn't pursue floral work or anything artistic early on in my career, though. When I left Bradley University (which was located in Peoria, where I grew up), I took a job as a flight attendant with United Airlines. I knew there was a whole world out there that I hadn't seen yet — and I wanted to start traveling and meeting new people. But in the back of my mind I still thought about flowers, and creating things. I moved to New York City for my first flight attendant assignment, and then I was transferred to San Francisco. I loved this job because I got to see every major city in the United States.

My travel came to a halt, though, soon after I met a handsome man in the U.S. Air Force test pilot school named Michael Clarke. We dated for five months and were married in November 1967, at which point I had to quit flying because back then flight attendants couldn't be married. It was difficult at first to give up my traveling career and to move far away from city life, but of course it was worth it to be with my husband.

We lived at Edwards Air Force Base, about seventy miles from Los Angeles, and I frequently drove to the L.A. flower market to buy flowers for our home. I didn't know a thing about floral design then — I just knew I liked flowers that looked pretty, smelled good, and had lots of petals. Some of my favorites were peonies, roses, and snapdragons.

After test pilot school, my husband was transferred

to Albuquerque, New Mexico, where I continued to experiment with flower arranging in my spare time, although I still didn't think I was doing it quite right. I also worked as a receptionist until our son, Chris, was born in December 1969. We moved to Montgomery, Alabama for a year, and then during the summer of 1971 we moved to Dayton, Ohio, where our daughter, Suzanne, was born in October. In Dayton, I started to play with flower designing more, and I began giving arrangements away to friends — because how many flower arrangements does one house need? It was fun to design things for other people, who seemed to like what I was making.

The Vietnam War was still going on, and when it was my husband's turn to go in 1974, he was stationed in Thailand to fly in Vietnam. I moved back to Illinois with my children to live with my mother, who was now alone because my father had recently died. I tried to get a job, even a part-time job, in a flower shop there, but no one would hire me because I didn't have any professional experience. Instead, I worked for a temporary employment agency and had an odd assortment of administrative jobs. At last the war ended, my husband returned, and we moved back to Dayton. I decided it was finally time for me to turn my flower arranging hobby into something more than a pastime, so I signed up for an adult night school class in home floral design. The teacher of the class owned a flower shop. "If you come to work for me," she told me when the class ended, "I'll teach you how to be a florist."

That sounded like a great idea to me, so I took a part-time job with her. She taught me a lot of basic designing, but I felt I needed more. While working in her shop, I learned that one of the top floral design schools in the

United States — Hixson's School of Floral Design — happened to be located in Ohio, in the Cleveland area. Although it was three hours away, I knew immediately that I wanted to go.

"Michael, I need you to stay with the kids for three weeks while I go to school," I announced to my husband one night in the spring of 1977. "I am going to floral design school in Cleveland."

He looked at me like I was nuts and asked, "Can't you find a school in Dayton?" Of course I could have, but I explained that this was one of the best schools in the country, and there was nothing like it nearby. He always supported my crazy ideas, and the craft projects I came up with but never got around to finishing, and he was supportive again this time. "Okay," he said. "Go for it." So I did. Chris was seven years old at the time and Suzanne was six, and neither of them knew quite why Mommy was leaving for a while, but it was just a few weeks, and they got over it pretty quickly. I lined up a sitter for them every day from the time that school ended until my husband got home, and off I went.

It was one of the best moves I ever made. I started to understand how to care for flowers properly, and I learned advanced design skills — color coordination, flower placement, and a variety of design approaches, from traditional to contemporary. I also learned I was a natural at making big, festive arrangements. "You're a party designer!" said the school's owner, Bill Hixson. "If your husband is ever stationed in Washington, you should see if you can volunteer as a designer at the White House." And he gave me the chief florist's name, which I carefully kept stashed in my wallet. Well, one year later, my husband *was* assigned to Washington, and I did call the chief florist. That was the beginning of my thirty-one-year career as a floral designer in the most important house in the country.

# Keeping the House in Bloom

T elephoning anyone to ask for a job can be intimidating — but calling the *White House* in search of employment, even a volunteer position, is downright nerve-wracking. My palms were sweating and my heart was beating fast on the afternoon in July 1978 when I dialed the main White House number and asked to be connected to Rusty Young, who was then the White House chief floral designer.

I had received Rusty's name more than a year earlier from Bill Hixson, the director of the floral design school I attended in Ohio. Bill had told me that if I ever found myself in Washington (a possibility, because my husband was in the military), I should call Rusty, whom Jacqueline Kennedy had hired in 1961 when she first established the Office of the White House Florist. It turned out that my husband did get a job in Washington, and we moved to the suburb of Fairfax, Virginia. So I decided to pick up the phone and see if they would be interested in having me work as a volunteer in the Carter White House. I kept telling myself that the worst they could say was "no."

An operator answered and transferred my call to the flower shop where, to my surprise, Rusty himself picked up the phone. "My name is Nancy Clarke," I said, hoping I didn't sound as nervous as I felt, "and I am a florist. I would love to volunteer to help you with anything you need." (Truly, I would have been happy to sweep floors or take out the garbage — and I did, many times.)

"Thank you for your call," Rusty said politely, "but we have plenty of volunteers at the moment." I'm sure he must have received dozens of phone calls like mine every month. When I eventually became chief floral designer, I got a steady stream of calls and letters all year long, and if a television special showed the Christmas decorations and mentioned our volunteers, I'd be slammed with inquiries for weeks. He tried to end the call by saying, "We'll keep your name on file in case anything opens up," but before he had a chance to hang up, I told him that I'd attended Hixson's School of Floral Design. He paused for a moment, realizing that I might legitimately be helpful. "I see," he said. "Would it be possible for you to come in for an interview next week?"

Little did I know at the time that this one phone call would lead to thirty-one years at the White House — with almost twenty-five of them as chief floral designer — and to relationships with six first ladies, from Rosalynn Carter through Michelle Obama. I served four of them — Nancy Reagan, Barbara Bush, Hillary Clinton, and Laura Bush — throughout their time in Washington, and developed wonderful, lasting, unique bonds with each one of them.

## My New Job

As I walked into the White House for my interview, my stomach was in knots — until I saw the White House Flower Shop. I was expecting something grand, elegant, and serene, but that was not at all what I encountered.

It was crammed, cluttered, and overrun with flowers, cut stems, and discarded leaves, and had refuse piled up. In other words, it was just like every floral shop I've ever been in. Rusty's three designers were hard at work in there, and everything felt so familiar that I relaxed immediately. Rusty's gentle demeanor also put me at ease. "Come in and sit down," he invited, and then kindly asked me about my design experience and the types of arrangements I'd made. When he realized how much experience I had with party flowers and funeral flowers (which tend to be large and elaborate), he asked when I would be available to work at the White House. I started as a volunteer the very next week.

On my first day as a volunteer, the very first thing Rusty told me was, "You cannot talk about what you see or hear in the White House outside of the White House." That was good advice — volunteers and staff members who didn't heed it were unceremoniously let go, and most members of the permanent staff took it quite seriously. Though (as I learned later) they did occasionally gossip amongst themselves when something really juicy was going on, they didn't tell the outside world about it — and they were very careful not to be loose-lipped around a brand-new volunteer.

Next I learned the unwritten rule of the flower shop: if you make an arrangement of flowers, you have to take it to where it goes. On my first day, Rusty asked me to put together an arrangement for the Library, a beautiful room on the ground floor with cream-colored walls, cream damask draperies, a pastel Oriental rug, and shelves filled with books about American history and culture that Jacqueline Kennedy had asked a committee to choose in 1963. The Library was the first "real" room I saw in the

White House. Until then all I'd really seen was the flower shop and the rather dingy, low-lit corridor leading to it. I was impressed — but I had no idea at that time how much more impressive the White House would become after the Reagans moved in.

Tour guests pass by the Library, so from Tuesday through Saturday (the days when public tours are held), there is always a grand arrangement there, on the center table. For the scale of the room and the table, I figured I needed to make an arrangement about forty inches in diameter, which would be the largest display I'd ever made. When I stepped into the refrigerator to select flowers, I felt like a kid in a candy store. I could take anything I wanted and use as much as I needed. After thinking about the cream and pastel color palette of the room and the stately furnishings, I decided to incorporate bright purple liatris, white chrysanthemums, pink lilies, and pale pink roses in a large china bowl with a delicate pattern. When it was finished, one of the designers told me it passed inspection, and it would be used for the tour the next day. I breathed a sigh of relief and became excited at the idea that an arrangement I made would be on display in the White House.

But first I had to get it into the Library, which I somehow managed to do without dropping it or splattering water anywhere along the way, though I felt the entire time I was carrying it that I was on the verge of losing it. A big, full arrangement — with the container full of wet foam, not to mention all the flowers — is unbelievably *heavy*. There were carts available to transport the arrangements, and I was tempted to use one. But I saw that all the guys in the shop carried their arrangements, and I wanted to prove that I could keep up with them. So I carried mine, too.

(Later on, when I was in charge of the shop, my staff and I most definitely used carts!)

Assigning me this arrangement to create was a quick test of my skill and ability to design in a style appropriate for the White House, not my personal style. And I handled the test well. The flower shop was staffed only by men at that time (floral designing was a male-dominated profession in the late '70s), but after the success of my first arrangement — and my placement of it! — I had the respect of everyone who worked there. After that, though I was still a volunteer, they had me designing pieces for public spaces and special events as if I were part of the staff. This was unusual for a volunteer, but the staff had realized that I could keep up with them and design high-quality pieces, so they made use of that.

For most of the year, the flower shop has a staff of four or five full-time employees, plus up to ten or eleven part-time people who work on an as-needed basis. Around the holidays, almost 100 additional volunteers, who are usually skilled commercial florists, come in to help the floral staff decorate the White House. I ended up working more hours than most volunteers — twenty to twenty-five hours per week, and more for big events.

I was strictly a volunteer until 1981, when I was hired first as a part-time staff member, and then full-time. Because I wasn't officially part of the staff in 1978, I did not work on flowers for the Carters' Residence, and I certainly didn't visit it. So I didn't even see the first lady until months after I'd started at the White House, and I only saw her occasionally after that. But in my years as a volunteer during the Carter administration, I did come to understand how the White House works behind the scenes.

## In the House

The White House, officially, is the residence and workplace of the president of the United States. Running such a grand and complicated building isn't easy, and there's a huge team that makes it all happen.

The White House itself is divided into three main sections: the Residence, the West Wing, and the East Wing. The first family lives in the rooms on the second and third floors of the Residence, which is the central and original part of the White House complex. They inhabit sixteen rooms plus bathrooms on the second floor, and twenty rooms plus bathrooms on the third floor — hardly cramped quarters. Both the second and third floors feature a central corridor, about twenty feet wide, which is divided into sitting areas. Most first families use the West Sitting Hall on the second floor as their main living room. Also on the second floor are the first family's kitchen, a dining room, and a beauty shop. The president and first lady's bedroom is on this floor, too, as are a few other bedrooms: some that the president's children might sleep in, the Lincoln Bedroom, and the Queens' Bedroom, which is named for the royal guests who have slept there, including queens of England, Greece, the Netherlands, and Norway. On the third floor are storage rooms and ten or eleven guest bedrooms, and above the third floor is a solarium that serves as an informal living and dining room.

The Residence staff has a hectic schedule on Inauguration Day, trying to get the new first family's clothes into their closets, their beds made, and their furniture unpacked. The staff also has to get rid of empty boxes and packing paper (which pile up all over), set up the Oval Office, prepare meals for the first family's guests, and put flowers in place for the family and all of their guests — and finish the whole job in less than five hours, before the family returns from the inaugural events.

Two or three times a year (around the holidays and definitely at inauguration time), all the guest rooms are filled, and at least one or two guest bedrooms are filled once or twice a week. We only placed flowers in the guest rooms when guests would actually be staying there, so on most days we had twelve to fifteen flower arrangements — not thirty-six — on the second and third floors. We almost always had arrangements for rooms on the second floor, including the sitting areas, the bedrooms, and the dining room. We always made sure the flowers in the first family's home coordinated with the colors in the rooms and looked like they belonged there, not like we were putting on a floral design show.

In the entire White House complex, there are 132 rooms and thirty-five bathrooms. Beneath the second floor in the Residence is the state floor, where you'll find the State Dining Room, which is used for state dinners; the East Room, where press conferences, large dinners, and after-dinner entertainment take place; and the Red, Blue, and Green Rooms, three parlors used primarily for cocktail parties and other receptions. Mrs. Reagan, whose favorite color was red, especially loved the Red Room, which had walls covered in red silk. She often had her official photographs taken in there.

Below the state floor on the ground floor are the Diplomatic Reception Room (one of four oval-shaped rooms in the White House, where diplomats enter the house before a state dinner, and which the president uses

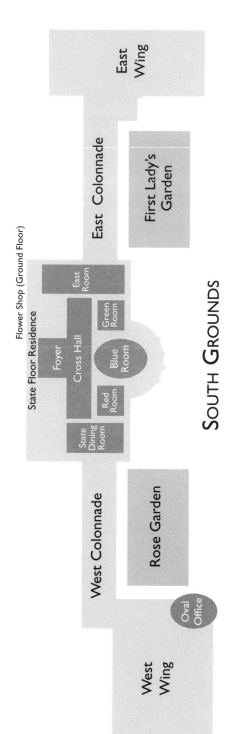

Pennsylvania Avenue

NORTH GROUNDS

Flower Shop (Ground Floor)

State Floor Residence

Foyer

Cross Hall

East Room

Green Room

Blue Room

Red Room

State Dining Room

East Colonnade

First Lady's Garden

East Wing

West Colonnade

Rose Garden

Oval Office

West Wing

SOUTH GROUNDS

Helicopter Pad

as his back door when he comes and goes to and from the helicopter on the South Grounds); the Map Room, a private meeting room that the first lady uses when she doesn't want people to come up to the second floor, and that members of the Residence staff can use for meetings as well; the China Room, where glass cases display presidential china plates; the Vermeil Room, a beautiful sitting room with glass cabinets showcasing sample gilded silver pieces from the White House vermeil collection; and the Library, which is often used for television tapings of interviews and public service announcements by the first family. These rooms, most of which visitors see during public tours, are on the south side of the ground floor. The rooms most visitors don't see — the main kitchen, the housekeeping office, the National Park Service office, the bowling alley, the carpenters' shop, and my home base, the flower shop — are along the corridor on the north side.

The president's Oval Office, the Cabinet Room, and the offices of the president's senior staff are all in the West Wing, while the offices of the first lady and her staff members are in the East Wing. Mrs. Carter was the first first lady to have a formal East Wing office, and she worked there almost every day.

Once I joined the flower shop as a full-time employee, I was part of the Residence staff, which includes more than ninety people, all there to look after the needs of the first family: the chef, pastry chef, calligraphers, curators, housekeepers, butlers, plumbers, electricians, and more. The entire Residence staff serves "at the pleasure of the president," which means someone can be let go at any time, for any reason, or for no reason at all. But because the Residence staff isn't political in nature, many, like me, remain on staff from administration to administration, regardless of whether the president is a Democrat or a Republican. Like most members of the Residence staff, I kept my political views to myself while I worked at the White House, and I still do.

The ushers are the leaders of the Residence team. Everything goes through the ushers' office, and the chief usher is the one in charge of it all — at the direction of the first family, that is — and the one in closest contact with the president and first lady. In Nancy Reagan's memoir, *My Turn*, she mentions that at the beginning of the Reagan administration, Letitia Baldridge (who had been Jacqueline Kennedy's chief of staff and social secretary) told her, "Make sure you get along with the chief usher . . . he runs the place. Next to your husband, he'll be the most important man in your life."

The chief usher when I started at the White House, and through the first term of the Reagan administration, after which he became White House curator, was Rex Scouten. (Mrs. Reagan did indeed think he was an important man in her life. She even named her Cavalier King Charles spaniel after him!) He had been at the White House in some capacity since 1949, when he became a Secret Service agent for President Truman, and he stayed for forty-eight years, until he retired in 1997. He was handsome, charming, and very old-school. Though I called all other members of the staff and subsequent chief ushers by their first names, he was always "Mr. Scouten." I call him that to this day.

When I was hired as a full-time floral designer in 1981, Mr. Scouten told me, "I'm not sure how it's going to work out having a woman as a floral designer — but we'll give it a try." But after that, he always supported me, and I loved working with him. When I checked in with him after state dinners to make sure things had gone well, Mr. Scouten didn't just say, "Yes, it was fine." Instead, he would put his arm around me and exclaim, "Well done!"

Mr. Scouten overheard me briefing my volunteers during my first Christmas season as chief floral designer. I assigned them to teams, told them exactly what they would be working on and where, and made sure everyone was well aware of what would be happening in every area of the house. He told me later, "That was great — this is the first time I'm *sure* Christmas will be well organized." (And after that Christmas, he gave me a raise.)

Once, when I presented Mrs. Reagan with a selection of samples and she didn't like any of them, Mr. Scouten assured me that I had nothing to worry about. "You can never please them during the third year of an administration," he said, and that proved to be true over the years. By the third year the first ladies are comfortable in their roles supervising the Residence staff, but they're starting to get tense or uneasy about an upcoming campaign or the prospect of leaving the White House. By the fourth year, they've adapted to whatever change is coming and they seem more relaxed.

When Mr. Scouten retired, Gary Walters became chief usher, and he served in that role until his retirement in 2007. Gary and I had a more collegial relationship — lots of joking, plenty of good-natured arguments, and much mutual respect. When my husband, who was still in the military, got orders to move to Korea and I told Gary I might be leaving the White House, he said quietly and sincerely, "Nancy, we'd really hate to lose you." He told me what an asset I was to the White House, and what a great job I was doing. His encouragement played a big role in my husband's decision to retire rather than go overseas, so we could stay in Washington and I could keep my job. I loved working with Gary as much as I loved working with Mr. Scouten, which was a good thing, because the chief usher was my day-to-day boss (though the first lady was my *real* boss).

Of course, when you work at the White House, you report to a lot of people. As chief floral designer, I also worked closely with the social secretary, who coordinates all White House social events, from luncheons with friends to the biggest state dinners. The social secretary was my first and main contact for every event. I made friends with all of the social secretaries I worked with through the different administrations, and I still keep in touch with many of them. Leading up to events, I spoke to them three or four or more times a day, and they often called me at home at night to tell me about little details that had changed for an event. There were generally one or two different social secretaries per administration, though Nancy Reagan and Laura Bush each had three. It's an intense job with incredibly long hours, and after a four-year stint, burnout tends to be inevitable. When a new social secretary starts, there's usually a month or two of overlap with the outgoing one, and during that period I would establish my working routine with them. My policy was to check in with them about everything and communicate frequently and openly. Every social secretary I worked with was very nice — it sounds sappy, but it's true. My volunteers always commented on how nice they were. Someone couldn't have that job if she weren't a nice person; a social secretary has to be friendly with everyone and roll with whatever comes her way.

The floral design staff works in parallel with the housekeepers and butlers to make the first family's Residence beautiful and to set up for events. It was always a little bit of a dance — I'd be placing flowers in the Residence while the housekeepers tried to make sure the floors were perfectly polished and I hadn't dripped any water. Or the butlers would wait for me to place a centerpiece on a dinner table before they would set it with china and glassware. Meanwhile, the executive chef and a team of four or five full-time staff and ten or more part-time chefs coordinated menus and prepared food for all events. The kitchen staff also prepared food for the first family's daily meals, which I was interested to learn the president and first lady pay for themselves. They can eat whatever they want, but only the food served at official functions is covered by the government. (Mrs. Reagan explained in her memoir that she was surprised by this, too, and was caught off-guard when she saw their first food bill. They also paid for incidentals like toothpaste and soap.) The president's valets handled such personal needs as shoe-shining, pressing clothes, carrying luggage, and so on. We were all on the same team, and we all had the same goal — to make the first family happy, every single day.

## A "Typical" White House Day

People often ask me to describe a typical day working in the White House. I have to tell them, of course, that there was no such thing as a typical day. Anything could happen — a luncheon for a queen, a dinner for a prime minister, a rock star playing a concert for hundreds of guests — and it usually did.

On a Monday in 1994 during the Clinton administration,

which came as close to "typical" as any, I got up at 4:20 a.m., as I did every morning. I had to be at work by 6:30, and before that I had to get dressed up (I wore a suit most days) and turn on the news to learn if anything important had happened in the political arena overnight that would affect us, or if any last-minute events or press conferences had been scheduled for inside the White House that day. If something big came up overnight that the ushers' office found out about, they'd alert me at home, but sometimes the press found out first and I would learn about it from the news before the ushers did. (I often heard about press conferences that hadn't yet been scheduled when I had left work the previous day. Once I learned about a pilot crashing a stolen plane into the White House; another time, I got the news about an armed intruder jumping a fence onto the South Lawn and wounding a Secret Service agent, who was a good friend of ours in the flower shop — luckily, he was fine.)

Press conferences in the Rose Garden fell outside my purview, but when they were held in the East Room or Cross Hall, I had to make sure fresh flowers were in place. After I caught up on the news — and drank a big cup of coffee — I drove the forty minutes (or longer, if something big was happening in Washington) from my house to the White House.

After parking near the East Wing on East Executive Avenue, which separates the White House from the Treasury Building, I showed my White House badge to get through two outdoor security checkpoints, and said hello to the officer stationed at the door where I entered the building itself. (This was before 9/11; after that there were even more layers of very stringent security.) I passed the visitors' office, which was really a reception room for guests. Because it was on my way, the first thing I did every morning was check the flower arrangement in the visitors' office — a large arrangement, often composed of flowers left over from dinners and other events, which we placed there to welcome visitors — so I could let my staff know if anything needed replacing or refreshing.

Then I went to the flower shop, where my staff was rolling in and grumbling about the early hour. It doesn't matter where you work — it's not very exciting to be there at 6:30 in the morning! I had a staff of three incredibly talented full-time designers at that time. Ronn Payne was a wonderful, very high-end designer who joked about everything and kept us entertained with his (sometimes off-color) stories. Keith Fulghum pushed us all to try new things by coming up with unusual color and flower combinations, which often worked beautifully. When Keith was in charge of the flowers in the Residence while George and Laura Bush lived there, I occasionally got a call from Mrs. Bush, who would tell me how much she liked the new direction we'd taken with the flowers. Wendy Elsasser, a fifth-generation florist, had worked in New York City with me on a Macy's window display project — we had turned the window into a lush garden, complete with "trees" made out of flowers. Wendy was funny and off-the-wall and often had me in stitches. I'd liked her immediately and was thrilled to hire her to join my staff because she was an excellent designer and a good friend.

On that Monday, as I did every day, I logged into the flower shop's computer and checked "Usher Information," which the ushers' office posted on the White House server, to see the schedule for the day. I saw nothing unexpected at that point. We had a huge congressional picnic on Tuesday evening in a tent on the South Lawn, but I'd ordered flowers for that the previous week, and my staff and I had worked over the weekend to begin assembling the 120 centerpieces. We'd have plenty of time today to finish them up, so we were in good shape. Luckily, no other big events were posted on the calendar that week. The president was going to be in the Oval Office all day (and not taking off or landing in the presidential helicopter, Marine One, since the South Lawn was unavailable while the tent was in place), so we were free to come and go to the tent as needed without being blocked by his motorcade. The National Park Service was taking care of arranging picnic tables in the tent, and Mrs. Clinton didn't have any last-minute events.

Since no emergencies loomed, I left the shop and took my daily tour through every public room in the White House where we kept flowers — three rooms on the ground floor and four rooms on the state floor, with one fairly massive arrangement in each room — and then checked in at the ushers' office to see if anything new had come up on the "Usher Information" schedule before I returned to the shop to divvy up assignments for the week. I rotated tasks weekly among my staff members. One would spend the week handling "tour pieces" (arrangements for public rooms that tours passed through; there were no tours on Mondays, so that's when we did the bulk of the work making and placing new displays for the tours that began just after 7:00 on Tuesday mornings), another would take care of the flowers in the West Wing, and another would oversee the flowers in the first family's Residence. I was in charge of flowers for special events. I also assisted my staff members with the daily maintenance as needed, and they assisted me with events. Working on the different types of arrangements didn't require different skills, but it did require working in styles and colors appropriate for the location. We rotated responsibilities for the sake of variety, so the same person didn't have to make an arrangement for, say, the Red Room every week.

By 10:00 a.m. my staff members were up to their elbows in flowers, making arrangements for their respective sections of the house, and I was checking in at the weekly meeting of all the Residence staff department heads. The meeting always included the chief usher (as well as the deputy usher on duty that day), the head butler, the executive chef, the head plumber, the head engineer, the curator, the National Park Service supervisor, the head carpenter, and me. The meeting, which was run by the chief usher, lasted anywhere from fifteen minutes to an hour, and we discussed all upcoming events for the week and any major events on the horizon.

As the meeting began that day, my mind drifted to finishing the arrangements for the congressional picnic. But I snapped back to attention when I heard Gary Walters, the chief usher, casually say, "And then we have 1,000 people coming for a picnic on Friday night." There had been no hint of *any* Friday event on the "Usher Information" schedule — let alone a picnic for 1,000 guests.

"Did I just miss something?" I asked in astonishment. "Gary, what are you talking about? What dinner?" It wasn't the size of the party that surprised me; the Clintons liked to entertain — a lot — and when they did, the events were often enormous. But usually I got more than a few days' notice for something this big.

Gary Walters explained that since the tent was up for the congressional picnic on Tuesday anyway, "the social office decided last night to keep it up and have a big press picnic on Friday evening." I started calculating the number of arrangements we'd need for 1,000 people — and then, trying to contain my alarm, I asked, "Gary, do you have a table count yet?" He shook his head. He had no other details. I wondered how much it was going to cost to expedite shipping in whatever flowers Mrs. Clinton wanted for the picnic. Gary knew what I was thinking. "Nancy," he chided me, as he often did, "whatever you have to do, don't spend too much money." I shot him a look — but didn't say anything.

As soon as the meeting ended, I ran to my shop to call the social office to talk to Ann Stock, Mrs. Clinton's social secretary. "Ann! I just heard about the picnic on Friday. What do you want us to do? I haven't ordered anything beyond what we need for the congressional picnic!"

"It's a picnic for the press," she explained calmly. "Let's just see if we can reuse some of the arrangements that are being used for tomorrow's picnic."

At tent events, guests ate off very simple rental china or paper plates, rather than pieces from the White House china collections, so I didn't have to worry about coordinating the look of the flowers with the place settings. For the Tuesday night picnic, we were assembling cheerfully casual arrangements of sunflowers mixed with bright yellow sunflower pom-pom chrysanthemums, and I wondered if they would work (and last long enough!) for the Friday evening event. When Ann stopped by our shop to see them a few minutes later, she simply said, in her upbeat way, "Oh, they'll be fine!"

We didn't have time to get Mrs. Clinton to okay them for Friday, but when a last-minute event came up, she was never picky about the flowers, so I knew if Ann said it would be fine, it would be.

Sunflower pom-pom chrysanthemums last like iron. I could leave them out on a counter for a week and they'd still look good. But we would have to replace any sunflowers that drooped. I knew local wholesalers would have these in stock. I quickly contacted seven or eight of them who could track down whatever I needed from all over the world. But in this instance, they wouldn't need to expedite any flower shipments from far away, which I knew would make Gary Walters happy.

I spent more than an hour on the phone with all my wholesalers, ordering replacement sunflowers to add to the arrangements for Friday. The main issue was that any sunflowers they delivered on Thursday had to be already open (sunflowers often arrive closed, and then it takes three or four days of water and sunshine to get them to burst open). I explained this to the wholesalers, and they knew me well enough to give me what I asked for. If a single flower arrived closed, it would go back on the next delivery truck and I wouldn't pay for it.

When we had Friday's details under control, my staff and I got to work finishing the table arrangements for the Tuesday picnic. Making 120 centerpieces is an assembly-line process. After the containers are prepared, one person puts in the sunflowers, the next person does the greens, and so on. There was no room in our shop for such an extensive project, so we worked on large tables outside in the alley behind our shop, using scaffolding as shelves to hold the finished arrangements, which were hardy enough to stay outside overnight. We finished — just barely — before the end of the day. Our standard working hours wrapped up at 3:30 p.m. — that's one benefit of coming in so early. We'd all worked over the weekend, and we knew we'd be working late the next day, so it was nice to have a reasonable nine-hour day.

Both picnics that week came and went with no remarkable problems. We quickly moved on to the next parties on our schedule, all the while keeping up with the everyday flowers in dozens of White House rooms. I remember stretches of three or four weeks (sometimes six, when the Clintons were the first family) when we had an event every day — dinners, concerts, luncheons, press conferences, and more — and I didn't get a single day off. Sometimes we also had to supply flowers for Air Force One and Camp David, too. The key to keeping up with everything without getting stressed was being extremely, meticulously well organized. Because that's how it was at the White House: frenzied work on special events was all part of the routine. However, there were some events — like a state dinner for the queen of England — that stood out and required extra special attention, and provided delightful memories for even the most experienced members of the White House staff.

## Royal Welcome: A State Dinner Fit for a Queen

State dinners at the White House are always a big deal. The president and first lady welcome a head of state from another nation to Washington, and the guest list might include government luminaries, former U.S. presidents and first ladies, Hollywood stars, and celebrated athletes. But the most memorable state dinner I ever worked on was the one we hosted on Monday, May 7, 2007, in honor of

Queen Elizabeth II of England. Not only was it the most formal and elaborate dinner I can recall — it was the *queen of England*. Yes, we had heads of state visiting the White House all the time, but most of us wouldn't have recognized many of them. Queen Elizabeth, on the other hand, was and is one of the most famous women in the world.

When a world-famous reigning monarch comes calling, of course she doesn't show up unannounced. It was January when I first heard that the queen *might* be visiting sometime in the spring. Amy Zantzinger, who had just started working

The President and Mrs Bush
request the pleasure of the company of

at a dinner in honor of
Her Majesty Queen Elizabeth II
and
His Royal Highness The Prince Philip
Duke of Edinburgh
to be held at
The White House
on Monday, May 7, 2007
at seven o'clock

White Tie                                    East Entrance

An invitation to the dinner in honor of Queen Elizabeth II and Prince Philip, May 7, 2007.

as Laura Bush's new social secretary, gave me the heads-up that it was a possibility, and told me not to breathe a word about it to anyone. She had no other details at that point, but wanted to share it with me because she was so excited. If it happened, it would be her first state dinner, and it would be a big one.

The official announcement to the White House staff about the queen's visit finally came in April. Our brand-new chief usher, Admiral Stephen Rochon, who came to the White House in March 2007 after Gary Walters retired, told us it would definitely be happening. And effective that instant, we were to be on alert. "Mrs. Bush wants the house to be absolutely spotless," he said. Well, Mrs. Bush always wanted the house to be in impeccable order. For this event, we were obviously taking it to a new level. In both the public and private areas of the White House, walls and woodwork were to be repainted, wooden doors were to be cleaned and polished, and all the hardware had to be buffed to a perfect shine. "If you see anything, *anywhere*, that needs attention, let the ushers' office know," he added. "Immediately."

Mrs. Bush didn't get visibly or vocally excited about things, but because she was giving so much attention to the queen's visit, I knew it meant a great deal to her. I heard from Amy that this would be a white-tie dinner, which is the most formal kind of dinner that the White House hosts. (President Bush didn't really want to wear white tie — he preferred less formal occasions — but when he and Mrs. Bush visited Buckingham Palace, the event in their honor was white tie, so it was appropriate to reciprocate.) It was the first and only white-tie dinner of the Bush administration, and the first and only time I worked on a white-tie dinner for a queen. It doesn't get any fancier!

As soon as I learned the dinner was on, I reached out to four of my part-time florists and put them on call. I knew my full-time staff and I would need their help during the three or four days leading up to the dinner. Then I started planning.

Although Mrs. Bush had been choosing bold, contemporary flower arrangements for recent dinners, Amy told me that the first lady wanted the flowers to be very formal, very classic, and very beautiful for the queen. I immediately thought of using pieces from the White House vermeil collection — elegant nineteenth century gold candelabras and wine coolers — as containers for the flowers. Mrs. Bush loved them, and they were the most formal (and most expensive!) in the White House.

In order to put together samples to show Mrs. Bush, I had to get a few vermeil pieces from the White House curators, a team of five or six full-time employees who oversee all the antiques and artwork in the house. The White House butlers take care of the frequently used china and other serving pieces, but the curators are ultimately responsible for everything that belongs to the White House, including china and crystal, and they kept the rare and valuable pieces under lock and key. The head curator was never thrilled when I asked to use pieces from the vermeil collection for flowers, because he was afraid they'd come back with water damage (which did sometimes happen). But all I had to say was, "This is what Mrs. Bush wants." He reluctantly gave me what I needed.

I presented samples to Mrs. Bush on April 24. Because we were using the vermeil containers, I thought the gold-

and-ivory Clinton china would look best, and I paired that with the vermeil flatware to show her. I made a few white-and-cream samples (with cream and white roses and white lilacs), and one sample with pale pink flowers. We set everything on a lush cream brocade tablecloth. Mrs. Bush came into the State Dining Room to see the samples and immediately chose the cream and white flowers, barely glancing at the pink. That's exactly what I thought she'd choose for this event, because they looked so classic and formal.

She told me she thought everything from the china to the flatware to the flowers was perfect. Her one request was that we keep the centerpieces very low, because the queen isn't very tall. "We want her to be able to see over them!" she said.

Once Mrs. Bush had approved the table setups, I quickly passed the information on to the ushers' office and to Cris Comerford, the executive chef. The chefs needed to know which china we were using for an event before they could finalize the menu, because not all china sets have the same pieces, and they needed to make sure they could serve all their menu items in the appropriate dishware. (When the chefs knew they wanted to serve a clear soup, for example, they'd ask me to steer the first lady toward the Reagan china, which includes the proper soup bowl.)

After I shared the tabletop plan with everyone, I brought Mrs. Bush's chosen samples with me back to the flower shop. I never threw samples away until after an event was over, even after the flowers withered and browned. The dead samples were my safety net. If anyone questioned what appeared on the tables at an event, I could point to the samples and explain that the first lady had signed off on them. The samples also gave me flower counts; I could look at the arrangements and know that each needed forty-two roses, or whatever the number was.

The very day Mrs. Bush approved the samples, I called the wholesalers and placed orders for roses (several varieties, in white and cream) and white lilacs. I ordered thousands and thousands of flowers, because not only would I be making thirteen centerpieces for the State Dining Room (one for each table of ten guests, with 100 roses in each), I also

*Dinner*
*in honor of*
*Her Majesty Queen Elizabeth II*
*and His Royal Highness The Prince Philip*
*Duke of Edinburgh*

*Spring Pea Soup with Fernleaf Lavender*
*Chive Pizzelle with American Caviar*
NEWTON CHARDONNAY "UNFILTERED" 2004

*Dover Sole Almondine*
*Roasted Artichokes, Pequillo Peppers and Olives*

*Saddle of Spring Lamb*
*Chanterelle Sauce*
*Fricassee of Baby Vegetables*
PETER MICHAEL "LES PAVOTS" 2003

*Arugula, Savannah Mustard*
*and Mint Romaine*
*Champagne Dressing · Trio of Farmhouse Cheeses*

*"Rose Blossoms"*
SCHRAMSBERG BRUT ROSÉ 2004

*The White House*                    *Monday, May 7, 2007*

The dinner menu for Queen Elizabeth II and Prince Philip, May 7, 2007.

needed to make arrangements for every room and hallway on the state floor as well as the second floor.

Flowers began arriving at the White House on the Thursday before the dinner — four days in advance. We cleaned each and every rose, cutting off the bottom leaves and thorns and recutting the stems, and placed them in water in our refrigerator to keep until we were ready to put them into arrangements. On Friday we prepped more than sixty containers for all over the house, cutting foam carefully to fit and inserting it, and fitting many containers with chicken wire to support heavy stems. On Sunday all my staff and I were at the White House for nine hours, assembling the flowers we needed in place on the state and ground floors for the queen's Monday morning arrival ceremony.

A camera crew from C-Span came in that day to film us working behind the scenes, getting ready for the dinner. This was unusual; we had been filmed a few times before for brief segments of National Geographic specials about the White House, but the flower preparation for most state dinners didn't attract that kind of attention.

I arrived at work at 6:15 on Monday morning and got right to work making the arrangements for the dinner itself. We made a few, then took them to the State Dining Room, in part to clear out some space in our shop, which was so small that storing flowers for large events was a nightmare, but also because I wanted to see how they looked in the room and make sure we were really happy with them. Luckily, we were.

We finished making the arrangements and, after the butlers placed the tablecloths and the housekeepers ironed them, we positioned the arrangements and put all the candles in the candlesticks and candelabras while the butlers wiped and polished the china, crystal, and flatware and set the tables. As always, there were a lot of people working in concert to prepare the room, and we had everything ready by 2:30 Monday afternoon, in time for the press preview.

About forty members of the press were allowed into the State Dining Room for a peek at the decorations and to interview Mrs. Bush. I always attended these previews, in case anyone had a specific question about the flowers or table settings. At the preview, Mrs. Bush introduced me, saying, "You've met her at all the Christmas previews and all the other previews. She's been here for many years, and once again, you can see her arrangements are just magnificent. They're just so perfect and elegant, I think, for Her Majesty." (It was very flattering, and I was happy to know she liked how the flowers looked when everything was set up.)

The preview lasted about fifteen minutes, and after that I spent the afternoon running around, double- and triple-checking every flower in every room, making sure everything looked fresh, and running back and forth to our shop if a blossom or leaf needed replacing. I did that until the guests began arriving at 6:30 p.m., at which point I finally had to stop and hope for the best! (Okay, I *almost* stopped — I didn't usually do this, but prior to this dinner I peeked into the State Dining Room one last time after the butlers had lit the candles, poured the water, and dimmed the lights, just before the actual dinner began. I wanted perfection, and I think we achieved it, or something very close to it. In the hushed stillness of the dining room before the guests arrived, the candle flames flickered, casting a warm glow on the gold vermeil centerpieces that held 100 white and cream roses each. The china and crystal sparkled, the flowers were gorgeous, and I must say the room looked spectacular.)

Speaking of guests, the attendees at this event included several all-star athletes, including golfer Arnold Palmer, quarterback Peyton Manning of the Indianapolis Colts, former NFL star Gene Washington (who was Condoleezza Rice's date), and Calvin Borel, the winning jockey from the Kentucky Derby, which had been run on the Saturday before the dinner, and which the queen — a horse racing fan — had attended. After he won, Mrs. Bush asked Amy, her social secretary, to call Calvin to invite him to the dinner. At first he thought it was a joke, but she finally convinced him it was a legitimate invitation from the White House. He happily accepted, but explained that he and his fiancée didn't have clothes for the occasion. Amy arranged to rent him a set of white tails, and shops in Louisville, Kentucky, home of the Derby, stayed open on Sunday so his fiancée could find a dress.

When guests — other than the guest of honor and a handful of select others — arrive for a state dinner, they come to the East Portico entrance to the White House and go first to the East Room for cocktails, by way of the Grand Staircase. A few very special guests, such as the vice president and the secretary of state, go to the Yellow Oval Room on the second floor to have cocktails and canapés with the guest of honor. Just sixteen guests joined the queen in the Yellow Oval Room prior to her state dinner.

For a state dinner, each minute (in some cases, increments of just a few seconds) of the evening is precisely orchestrated, and there is a detailed, printed schedule outlining every step so staff members know exactly what should be going on, and when. On the night of the queen's dinner, at 7:15, on Amy's cue, the Yellow Oval Room guests, except for the "four principals" (President and Mrs. Bush and Queen Elizabeth and Prince Philip), were escorted to the East Room by the chief of protocol and announced in protocol order.

At 7:20, the "four principals" left the second floor and descended the Grand Staircase to the Cross Hall while "Hail America" played. They paused (for "5 to 10 seconds," according to the schedule) at the bottom of the stairs for a photo opportunity, then went to greet the East Room guests in a receiving line. The receiving line concluded promptly at 7:55, and at 8:00 on the dot, President Bush delivered a toast to greet guests. The queen gave her toast immediately after. At 8:10, dinner was served.

When the dinner started in the State Dining Room, my staff and I were still at the White House, working with the operations staff to transform the East Room from a cocktail site into an entertainment venue. Violinist Itzhak Perlman would be playing for the queen and all the guests after dinner. As the operations guys were moving tables and we were replacing flower arrangements, Chief Usher Rochon stopped in to tell me that when the entertainment concluded, the queen wanted to meet the staff members in charge of getting the dinner ready before she left the White House. So, he said, I should change into my gown. "Gown?" I asked. "I don't have one here," I said, explaining that I'd never needed one before.

"What do you mean you don't have a gown at work?" He was incredulous and insisted that I go talk to Amy immediately. When I found her, Amy looked over my black suit, silk shell, and pearls, and told me not to worry. "Just stand with your legs together, and no one will notice," she said.

We finished setting up the East Room, and the rest of my staff left at 8:30 p.m., but I stayed to meet the queen and got a head start on cleaning up our shop, which we'd torn apart in the process of getting ready for this dinner.

About a dozen staff members formed a receiving line to greet the queen as she emerged from the Perlman performance around 11:00 p.m. I'd been working at the White House for almost twenty-nine years at that point, and I had met many celebrities, so I wasn't nervous. But I was definitely more excited than usual, because it was the queen of England. I was also very tired, which took some of the edge off for me. Moments before we met her, the queen's aide — known as her "gentleman" — briefed us on how to behave. "Do not speak to her unless she speaks to you," he told us. "Do not extend your hand to her. Wait for her to put her hand out first. And," he added, "do not attempt to touch the queen."

I learned later that when Calvin Borel, the Derby-winning jockey, posed for a photo with the queen and Mrs. Bush, he affectionately put his arms around both of them. It was a complete breach of protocol, but it was so sweet and he was so excited that no one seemed to mind.

Though I worked for the most famous couple in America and had met plenty of celebrities, meeting the queen left me star-struck. She wore the Queen Mary tiara, which her grandmother had given to her, as well as a diamond necklace known as the Festoon, and diamond earrings. Her gown was creamy white with a beaded bodice and chiffon skirt, and over it she wore the blue Order of the Garter sash. I was amazed that someone so petite and delicate, with such a soft smile, could look so grand and regal. She did not speak to me, but she did extend her hand (it was tiny!), and I took it for a brief handshake — one of the most memorable of my life.

Mrs. Bush, who followed Queen Elizabeth and Prince Philip through the staff receiving line, looked beautiful in an embroidered turquoise silk faille dress with a matching bolero jacket by Oscar de la Renta. As she greeted me, she whispered happily, "The flowers were *perfect.*" The next morning the *Washington Post* called the dinner "the most elegant Washington evening in a decade."

When I finally left to go home that night after the long, exhausting day, I walked toward my car in the pitch black feeling elated and satisfied. I knew how gorgeous the event had been — and I could tell how much it had pleased Mrs. Bush. Pleasing the first lady was more important to me than anything else.

# My First *First Lady: Rosalynn Carter*

*The flowers in the White House were a joy for me every day. The staff in the flower shop was superb, and an army of volunteers, floral specialists from all over the country, made their very challenging job possible. Nancy herself started as a volunteer for us in the summer of 1978, later assumed a full-time position, and remained through five more administrations.*

*Nancy and the other White House florists worked hard to get to know the style of each president and first lady and very soon learned the kind of flowers and arrangements we liked. They knew I was partial to roses, and we almost always had some roses in the family quarters as well as the guest areas. When we were hosting visiting heads of state, they worked with the social secretary and the State Department to find out which flowers would be especially meaningful for our guests. For instance, when we were planning for the visit of Prime Minister Deng Xiaoping of China, we learned that the camellia originated in China. So we had friends at home in Georgia bring hundreds of these flowers to us. The camellias were used throughout the White House and in low arrangements surrounded by votive candles as centerpieces for the state dinner. I think one of my favorites and one of the most beautiful of the time we were there was when the king and queen of Belgium visited for a luncheon. Nancy helped decorate long tables in the East Room with dogwood boughs loosely arranged in vermeil containers.*

*For three decades, Nancy showcased her talent and creativity to the delight of people from all over the world. Her contributions helped convey the beauty of our nation and the warmth of our citizens to everyone who entered the president's house.*

*— Rosalynn Carter*

45

**I** 'll never forget the first time I met Mrs. Carter. I was a volunteer for the floral staff during the Carter administration, not a full-time staff member, and so I never went to the first family's Residence. It wasn't until months after I first started working at the White House that I even laid eyes on Mrs. Carter. Though I became quite close to the next four first ladies who inhabited the White House, this was my first time seeing a first lady in person. Our initial encounter was at Christmastime, just after the floral staff and volunteers had finished putting in long hours to get all the holiday decorations in place. I had worked many extra hours, making bows for all the wreaths, helping to decorate the main Christmas tree in the Blue Room, assisting with putting together handmade garlands, and assembling mantel flower arrangements for the East Room.

For each Christmas at the White House, there is a theme to the decorations; that year the theme was "antique toys." It was sweet and nostalgic, and it brought back treasured memories of Christmases from my childhood, when I made candles with my grandparents and placed them in the fireplace and on tables around the house. Though the White House celebrates Christmas on a grand scale, my favorite kinds of decorations are the simple cutout paper ornaments that my children used to make when they were young. I have kept them through the years and still hang them on our family tree every Christmas. Though I thought the decorations for my first Christmas at the White House were extensive, I had no idea how much more elaborate Christmas would become in the next decade!

Mrs. Carter wanted to thank the volunteers for our hard work, so a group of us gathered in the Grand Foyer to say hello to her. Prior to that day, I'd only seen first ladies on television, so the idea of meeting one in person was a thrill. She was arguably the most famous woman in the country, and there's an aura of majesty around anyone in that role. Working at the White House was part of my routine by this point, but every day still held a dose of excitement and anticipation for me — I was working in the same building with the president and the first lady, and even though it hadn't happened yet, there was always a chance I could see one of them face-to-face. The mere possibility of that made every day thrilling.

In case that happened, all staff and volunteers are briefed on appropriate behavior for first family interactions. It's not as complicated as protocol for meeting royalty (as I later learned), but I was instructed to refer to the first lady as Mrs. Carter, and President Carter as Mr. President. When responding to questions, I was to say "Yes, ma'am" or "No, sir." I was never to interrupt them if they were speaking to someone or doing something, and I was to step back to let them pass if they were coming down the hall.

I felt a rush of adrenaline as Mrs. Carter came around the corner, and I could feel myself blushing. She looked prettier in person than she did on television. She was dressed simply in a blouse and a skirt, and a fashionable-at-the-time wide belt. She didn't speak to me directly, nor I to her, but I remember thinking when I saw her how stylish she looked, and that I definitely needed to get some wide belts. From then on I found that my personal style was influenced by whichever first lady I was working for at the time. They were such iconic, lovely figures, and it was hard not to want to mimic their look.

Mrs. Carter was calm and down-to-earth, and she spoke to the volunteers simply and sincerely, with her slight southern accent. "Thank you so much for your help," she said. "The decorations are lovely, and Jimmy and I appreciate what you did for us." I believed she really was appreciative, especially when I saw her at the Christmas party for the Residence staff and regular volunteers a week or so later. She was at the party chatting with all the guests and serving eggnog and cider to us. She was the only first lady I ever saw do that. She did it at the staff party every year, and I thought it was so considerate. (Although the next year, my daughter, who was only seven at the time, was accidentally served multiple glasses of alcoholic eggnog — by a few different butlers, not by Mrs. Carter — and when we left the party she was a little tipsy!)

## Floral Exam

I didn't see Mrs. Carter frequently after that Christmas, but every month or so I was in the room when she came to look at floral samples for a dinner or party. Gretchen Poston, Mrs. Carter's social secretary, generally showed Mrs. Carter the samples that the flower shop staff or guest designers had made, and I was occasionally there to help Gretchen carry things. During that time, I learned from Gretchen and Rusty what was involved with planning flowers for White House events. As soon as the flower shop staff learned about an upcoming occasion, the chief floral designer would talk to the social secretary about what sort of arrangements we should be thinking about — colors, size, level of formality, and any restrictions.

For a state dinner for President Junius Richard Jayawardene of Sri Lanka, during the Reagan administration, the social secretary let us know that the office of protocol at the State Department had told her

In my first year as a volunteer floral designer at the White House, I was delighted to assist with the arrangements for the state dinner for King Hussein and Queen Noor of Jordan on June 17, 1980.

I probably spent more time in the White House flower shop (creating flower arrangements for state dinners, Christmases, Camp David, and even Air Force One) than I did at home.

Sometimes we had so many arrangements that we needed to work in the alley outside the flower shop. Here my part-time staff members Wayne Maness and Martha Blakeslee and I are getting ready to move these lush yet informal centerpieces of 'White Marguerite' daisies to the South Lawn for a congressional picnic in June 2006.

Early in my career as a volunteer floral designer, I was sometimes nervous because I always wanted my arrangements to be perfect! I was lucky to learn from experienced guest designers who were brought in by the first ladies to create displays at the White House. Here I'm preparing a centerpiece for an April 1980 luncheon for the king and queen of Norway.

Here I'm in a refrigerated truck on the South Grounds, unloading centerpieces for the historic Camp David Peace Accords dinner, celebrating the peace treaty between Israel and Egypt that was signed on March 26, 1979.

At the Camp David Peace Accords dinner, President and Mrs. Carter (center) sat with Prime Minister Menachem Begin of Israel (right).

Prime Minister Masayoshi Ohira of Japan requested barbecue, one of his favorite meals, for his state dinner on May 4, 1979. To accompany the relaxed culinary theme, we created centerpieces using clay pots filled with begonias.

Here President Carter is in deep discussion with Prime Minister Margaret Thatcher of England (left), at a state dinner in December 1979. The red flowers in the centerpiece seem to match the red dress that Mrs. Carter (right) is wearing.

My daughter, Suzanne, and my son, Chris, attended their first Christmas staff party at the White House in December 1979. I have to admit that they were never quite as excited about this annual event as I was.

My husband, Michael, with Chris and Suzanne posed for a picture after leaving a White House staff Christmas party. The kids were troupers for going every year, especially since there weren't many activities at the party for young children.

I always admired the way Mrs. Carter made an effort to serve coffee to volunteers at the White House staff Christmas party in December 1979, as she did every year. She was the only first lady to do this — and she even served punch to my kids.

In the Carter era, walk-throughs of the Christmas decorations were extremely casual. One day, Mrs. Carter just popped in and invited another volunteer, Mary Pamplin, and me to accompany her as she viewed the different rooms. Behind us is Chief Usher Rex Scouten.

Rusty Young, the White House chief floral designer, had an excellent eye when it came to floral displays. He gave me the chance to volunteer at the White House — and started me on my career there!

This is the beautiful Green Room, one of three parlors at the White House where cocktail parties and receptions are held. We picked up on the accent colors in each room for our floral arrangements.

The Cross Hall is enormous and stately, and it was always an exciting challenge to decorate it for Christmas.

One year at Christmastime the park service installed poinsettia trees in the majestic Cross Hall. To add to the festive look, we created garlands of natural sugar pinecones, red pepper berries, large swirly glass balls, red glass balls, red glass grapes, and gold and white lights.

This is the China Room, where I sometimes met with first ladies to explain decorating ideas. Here I'm talking with Mrs. Clinton; behind me is Chief Usher Gary Walters, and on the right is Social Secretary Ann Stock.

The Vermeil Room, which is also called the Gold Room, features portraits of seven first ladies, including Lady Bird Johnson (right) and Jacqueline Kennedy (left).

The White House Library, shown here with a red floral arrangement, showcases a chandelier that once belonged to the family of author James Fenimore Cooper.

Because of the intense shade of blue in the Blue Room, we had to find striking blue flowers, and other flowers in rich complementary shades, that wouldn't be overpowered by the décor.

This is a view through the East Colonnade toward the East Wing, where the first lady and her staff have their offices. The heat from the sun dried the holiday wreaths we put there, and we had to replace them every ten days.

The distinguished Rex Scouten was the chief usher when I started working at the White House. To this day, I call him "Mr. Scouten."

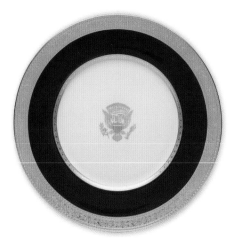

Wilson China Pattern

FDR China Pattern

Truman China Pattern

Eisenhower China Pattern

Johnson China Pattern

Reagan China Pattern

Clinton China Pattern

Bush China Pattern

These eight china patterns span presidencies from the Wilson administration to the George W. Bush administration. The most popular patterns for state dinners while I worked at the White House were the red Reagan china and the gold Clinton china, which coordinated well with a wide variety of color schemes.

The East Room is often used for press conferences, large dinners, and after-dinner entertainment. When ballet star Mikhail Baryshnikov danced here, he once leapt so high he hit a chandelier!

Rich red silk adorns the walls of the Red Room, where intimate dinners are occasionally held.

not to use *any* blue, because blue was the color of the political party opposing the incumbent head of state. There were also general restrictions: we needed to be careful about using white since in Muslim and many Pacific Rim countries, this color is reserved for funerals. In some Central and South American countries, the same is true of the color yellow. Sometimes it's the type of flower that must be avoided; in certain countries and regions, lilies, mums, or carnations are used only for funerals. In later years I researched the flowers, fruits, and flag colors of whichever country we were honoring with a state dinner, to see if I could incorporate any elements into the arrangements.

After Gretchen and Rusty had their initial conversation, she would stop by the flower shop to chat quickly about our options, then a designer would get to work making a sample arrangement. During the Carter administration, the floral designers would usually prepare only one sample, sometimes two. When I took over, I always made three samples, to give the first lady a real choice, but not so many choices that she would be overwhelmed.

When the sample was ready, Gretchen would find a time slot in the first lady's schedule and take the flowers — along with a coordinating tablecloth and china, crystal, and flatware option — and set everything up on a table in the room where the event would be held. The first lady would come to look at it, and if she liked it, we'd order the flowers we needed for the actual event. As far as I knew, Mrs. Carter never rejected a sample. The first option was always fine with her. Mrs. Reagan, on the other hand, often said, "I think I would like something different," and we would have to create something new and find another time to show it to her — which is why, after I took over, I always prepared more than one sample for the initial preview.

Mrs. Carter was actively involved with President Carter's administration, attending cabinet meetings, representing him officially on trips abroad, and chairing the President's Commission on Mental Health. She didn't seem to get too caught up in event planning, which may be why she rarely, if ever, asked anyone to create new sample arrangements for her.

Compared to first ladies I later worked with, Mrs. Carter had simple, understated tastes. The dinners she hosted, especially in comparison to dinners I worked on for subsequent first ladies, were fairly informal, and the gowns she wore to formal events weren't usually beaded or dramatic. Once she held a state dinner in honor of the prime minister of Japan outside on the terrace overlooking the Rose Garden, and because the prime minister was a fan of barbecue, she asked the chefs to serve barbecued buffalo and chicken that they cooked over open pits. The table centerpieces were clay pots of begonia plants surrounded by hurricane candles — nothing fancy at all, but perfect for an outdoor barbecue. It was by far the most casual state dinner I ever worked on.

Mrs. Carter often invited guest floral designers from the Washington, D.C. area to the White House to create arrangements for state dinners. I'm not sure how Rusty felt about that, but he was such a gentleman that he would never have voiced a complaint. And when you work at the White House, if the first lady wants you to do something, you just do it. (That's your job, after all!) Besides, a little extra help is generally a good thing, because getting ready for an event can be hectic. The guest designers' arrangements often had a looser, more contemporary feel than the formal, elaborate arrangements I'd seen in pictures of White House events from earlier administrations.

One of the guest designers who came to the White House frequently during the Carter administration was Dottie Temple, who ultimately took over as chief florist for Rusty when he retired in 1981. She was a terrific designer with a great sense of style, and I learned an incredible amount about high-end design working for her. We also cracked each other up, and often laughed until tears rolled down our faces. Once we were together waiting to go into a luncheon at the Press Club, and we were laughing so hard about something that a waiter asked us if we'd been drinking. (No, we hadn't.) Dottie was the one who hired me as a part-time staff member in March 1981, and then full-time in November 1981 when she needed to replace a full-time designer. When Dottie retired in 1985, I was promoted to chief floral designer.

Even the most elaborate dinner Mrs. Carter hosted — a sit-down dinner for 1,300 in honor of the Camp David Accords (the peace agreements signed in 1978 by Egyptian President Anwar Sadat and Israeli Prime Minister Menachem Begin) — featured casual centerpiece arrangements of yellow forsythia and cheery yellow tulips on a floral tablecloth; white wine and champagne were chilled in Sears, Roebuck and Co. fishing boats that served as ice buckets. This may have been due in part to the fact that the United States was in a recession during the Carter administration, and the Carters chose to be conservative in their spending on flowers. Many flowers were donated and/or came from cuttings we took from the roadside (legally, from roads maintained by the National Park

Service) or from the White House farm in Maryland. Mrs. Carter's favorite flowers were the kinds that grew in her own backyard in Georgia — white camellias and roses. We reused every single flower down to its dying day.

No matter how formal or simple, each event I worked on during the Carter administration was awe inspiring to me. It was all so new. I had never seen anything like a state dinner for a head of state, or a tented dinner for more than a thousand guests. The sheer quantity of flowers was staggering, and so was the quality. The flowers the White House used were more beautiful than any I'd ever worked with. And, of course, knowing who the guests would be was mind boggling. When President Sadat and Prime Minister Begin pulled into the White House driveway in their limos for the Camp David Accords dinner, I was standing about fifteen feet away from the cars. I felt like I was watching history in the making.

## Meeting and Greeting

I had only one conversation with President Carter, and it was very short, but still, it was a conversation with the *president*. I was going through a receiving line at a staff Christmas party in 1980. When you go through a receiving line, an aide introduces you to the president and announces who you are. As the aide was announcing me, I was a bundle of jitters. What would he say? What would I say? President Carter simply shook my hand and asked, "How do you like working in the flower shop?" to which I replied, "I love it." And that was it. I was glowing for the rest of the day.

I didn't keep in touch with Mrs. Carter after she left the White House, but when she came to visit Mrs. Obama, soon before I retired, I had lunch with her. The night before, the ushers' office called me at home to say, "You have a luncheon tomorrow." I thought they meant I needed to arrange flowers for a luncheon, but no, they meant that I was one of the guests! It was just Mrs. Carter, Bill Allman (an assistant curator during the Carter administration), and me. When Mrs. Carter arrived at the White House, Bill and I met her in the Diplomatic Reception Room and escorted her to the Old Family Dining Room. The three

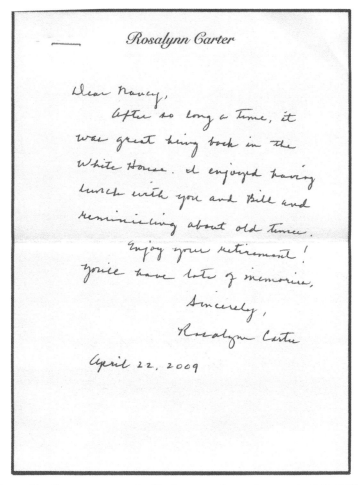

A note Mrs. Carter sent to me after I had announced my retirement, April 22, 2009.

of us sat at the end of the large table. "It's so good to see you after all these years," she said, in her soft accent that hadn't changed a bit. "You look wonderful," I told her, and she really did. She told us stories about the work she had been doing with care-giving organizations and the terrible conditions some of the world's children are living in and how desperately they needed our help. I was so thrilled to be sitting with her that I'm not even sure I ate — I certainly don't remember what we had for lunch. After lunch, Bill and I walked her into the Blue Room and waited with her, and as Mrs. Obama came down the hall to greet her, Bill and I gave her big hugs and slipped away. A few weeks later, she came to visit Mrs. Obama again; after their meeting she asked where I was, but nobody could find me, so she left. I was so sorry to miss her, but overjoyed that I did have the opportunity to become reacquainted with my first first lady.

# A Return to Grandeur: Nancy Reagan

*I have always loved flowers, and I kept my home full of them. So Nancy and I had something in common from the beginning, and I liked her right away. We worked closely together for eight years, and she was always fun and wonderful to be around. We developed a close personal friendship, one that I cherish.*

*While I like all flowers, peonies are my favorites. Whenever we had a dinner at the White House, I always said, "Let's have peonies." And usually, Nancy would have to gently remind me, "Peonies only bloom in May, Mrs. Reagan." Because Nancy was so creative and talented, she always designed an alternate arrangement that I loved. But it was such a joke between us that when I left the White House, Nancy presented me with a pillow embroidered with the words, "Peonies Bloom in May." I treasure that pillow to this day.*

*— Nancy Reagan*

"**O**nce you're in the White House," Nancy Reagan warned future first ladies in a speech she gave close to the end of the Reagan administration, "don't think it's going to be a glamorous, fairy-tale life. It's very hard work with high highs and low lows. Since you're under a microscope, everything is magnified."

That's true, but I think it was especially true for Mrs. Reagan, who attracted quite a bit of attention even by first lady standards. Her flair for fashion, her redecoration of the White House, her particular personality, and her adoration of her husband were among the topics that the press and public latched onto. The Reagans also dealt with quite a bit of personal turmoil — from the assassination attempt on the president to cancer diagnoses for both of them — which drew plenty of interest.

The Reagans' entrance to the White House coincided almost exactly with my transition from volunteer to staff member, which meant that I worked in the private Residence as well as the public rooms and saw Mrs. Reagan much more often than I saw Mrs. Carter. Mrs. Reagan was generally friendly but reserved with the staff, and our relationship became closer slowly, more so after I became chief floral designer.

I first met Mrs. Reagan a few days after she moved into the White House, while I was assisting Dottie Temple, who was chief floral designer from 1981 until I took over in 1985. Dottie had a big personality, and I laughed often at her quips and comments. Once when she placed an arrangement of willow branches in the Reagans' bedroom, President Reagan suspiciously eyed them and asked, "About those sticks on the mantel. Is anything going to happen to them?" Without missing a beat, Dottie replied, "Yes, sir. I'm going to get rid of them as soon as possible."

Though she worked all week in Washington, Dottie's home was in the Boston area and she commuted there on the weekends. She missed her husband and the rest of her family, so she resigned at the end of President Reagan's first term. Mrs. Reagan's interior designer, Ted Graber, and I had become close friends while I was working with Dottie. Unlike the protocol in other administrations with which I worked, I dealt with Ted far more often than I did with Mrs. Reagan's social secretaries, because (at Mrs. Reagan's request) he took a lead role in planning and designing all events. Once Dottie had given her notice, I assumed they would bring in a famous designer as chief. But one night, as a dinner was taking place on the state floor, Ted asked me to come to the solarium to talk with him. I thought he was going to tell me who the new designer was going to be, but instead, he interviewed me for the job. He asked me questions about how I would do things and different styles of flowers I would use for dinners. Then he offered me the position. I was thrilled and totally shocked. Suddenly I was going to be responsible for everything from floral decorations to Christmas designing. It was exciting — and scary.

But in my early years as a floral design staff member, I didn't dream that would ever happen. I was just thrilled to be working at the White House. I'll always remember the first time I saw Mrs. Reagan in person. It was 1981 and I was helping Dottie with a sample setup. When Mrs. Reagan walked into the room, I was surprised at how small she was. I knew she was petite and thin, but I didn't expect her to be quite so tiny — although she did exercise almost every day, and she was quite fit and strong. I also didn't expect her to be so beautiful. Though she looked lovely in photographs, in person, her face was really stunning — more than pictures ever showed, I think.

Whenever I happened to catch a glimpse of Mrs. Reagan her clothes were immaculate, whether she was in a jogging suit on her way to exercise first thing in the morning, or in a dress or an elegant gown. She often wore beautiful suits and silk blouses, by extremely high-end designers as far as I could tell. She inspired me to buy classic suits and to dress up more, so much that one of the butlers said to me,

"My God, you're starting to dress like Mrs. Reagan!" I took that as a compliment, because I thought she dressed beautifully. Red was her favorite color, and she wore it often. Her gowns for dinners and other formal occasions were elaborate and glamorous, and I always peeked out of the ushers' office to get a glimpse of her as she descended the Grand Staircase before an event began, so I could see what she was wearing.

## Cleaning Up the House

Before the Reagans even came to Washington in 1981, everyone working at the White House had a feeling things were going to change. They were a Hollywood couple, and the press played up their movie star friends and Mrs. Reagan's fashionable clothes. We were eager to learn what their arrival would mean for us and for our daily routines.

One of the biggest things that changed during the Reagan administration was the White House itself. When she moved in, Mrs. Reagan wrote in her memoir, she was "dismayed" by the state of disrepair the house was in, especially the private rooms in the Residence. I never entered those rooms when the Carters lived there, but Mrs. Reagan described bedrooms that hadn't been painted in twenty years, cracks in the walls, and a Center Hall (the wide corridor that first families began using as their main living area) that was "virtually empty."

When a new first family moves into the White House, Congress allots them a budget of $50,000 to refurbish the home. However, the Reagans didn't take this money; instead, they raised more than $800,000 in private donations to update and decorate their living space. Ted Graber, Mrs. Reagan's interior decorator from California, came to the White House — he actually lived there for almost a year in a guest bedroom on the third floor — and helped her revamp the house. (The *New York Times* described his style as "Hollywood traditional, traditional with a flamboyant edge.") They pulled dozens of pieces of historical furniture and mirrors that belonged to the White House out of storage and had them restored so they could be used again. A reproduction Sheraton sofa, *bergère* chairs, and an upholstered Chippendale-style bench, all of which had been languishing in the White House storage facility, were used in the Center Hall. Mrs. Reagan and Ted chose a beautiful pale yellow paint color that brightened the walls of the Center Hall considerably; I remember waiting for her on the second floor to show her a sample and watching the painters use a careful striation technique in which they layered glaze over paint and then combed through the glaze to create a lovely texture. They also refinished the floors and mahogany doors, cleaned every fireplace in the White House (there are twenty-nine!), and updated kitchens and bathrooms.

The results of the renovations were truly gorgeous, and while many people appreciated what she did — Speaker of the House Tip O'Neill apparently said to President Reagan, "Please tell Nancy that I've never, ever, seen the White House look this beautiful" — she caught a lot of flack from the press for it, too.

Mrs. Reagan was startled by the negative feedback, but she didn't apologize. She explained in her memoir, "I did want to reclaim some of the stature and dignity of the building. I've always felt that the White House should represent this country at its best. To me, this was so obvious that I never dreamed I would be criticized for my efforts."

When Mrs. Reagan was getting ready to host her first Governors' Dinner, she was surprised to find out that the White House did not have a full set of china. Lady Bird Johnson had been the only first lady since the Truman administration to order china, but her set didn't include finger bowls, dessert bowls, or bouillon cups. The china's relatively informal pattern, with a band of wildflowers around the outside, is probably more appropriate for a ladies' luncheon than a state dinner (although Barbara Bush, an avid gardener, loved it and used it almost exclusively, even for formal dinners).

Each first lady has the option to select new china, which becomes part of her legacy to the White House; however, not all first ladies do. Because Barbara Bush liked the Johnson china so much, for example, I don't think she thought new china was necessary. The cost of china purchases is covered either by donations or by private funds from the White House Historical Association, the White House Endowment Trust, or the White House Historical Trust. Today there are many White House china patterns, but only a few sets are used on a regular basis. (Some are considered priceless, while others have too few pieces to be used for most White House dinners.) Among the most frequently used china patterns while I worked at the White House were the Wilson base plates and the FDR china, which Mrs. Clinton often used together, and filled in with enough pieces to make a complete formal dinner service; the Truman china; the Johnson china, which Lady Bird Johnson designed to showcase American wildflowers; the Reagan china, which has 220 place settings; and the Clinton china, which has 300 place settings. Laura Bush also selected new china, but it wasn't introduced until January 2009, just two weeks before President Bush left office.

Mrs. Reagan wanted more stately china than the Johnson pattern, so we used a mix of patterns for the Governors' Dinner. We had to do this often before she ordered a new set because we didn't have a single set large enough for an entire large dinner. She quickly ordered 220 settings of an elegant red-banded china with a raised gold presidential seal, designed by Lenox. We called the shade of red she chose "Reagan red" when we were matching flowers to it, because it had a slight cast of orange rather than blue. The press pounced on this as another example of her profligate spending and extravagance, but the funds for the china were actually donated — she didn't spend taxpayers' money on it. And I really think the White House needed it. I can tell you that once we had the Reagan china, it got plenty of use, and planning for large dinners became much easier. President Truman's daughter, Margaret Truman Daniel, defended the new china to the *New York Times*, saying, "I think it's too bad about this hassle over her doing something she should have done. It's really ridiculous. As for mixing up place settings from different settings bought by different administrations . . . all I can say is that it looks just awful."

Flowers are one area where the White House certainly did become more extravagant when Mrs. Reagan became first lady. Ted Graber, her interior decorator, taught us a lot about what she liked: lush, abundant, full arrangements that reminded me of vibrant California gardens. We started using more of everything. More flowers per arrangement, and more arrangements in general. More lilies, amaryllis, freesia, tulips, and hydrangeas. Plus, in the early 1980s, the U.S. started using air freight to import flowers, and it became feasible to get flowers from all over the world — Europe, Africa, New Zealand, South America — so suddenly we could use a lot of varieties that we didn't have access to before. But it was really Mrs. Reagan who set the tone and, I think, changed White House flowers forever. Every first lady since then has continued in the same vein, and we never retreated to the sparse look of the Carter years. After I became chief floral designer, a butler let me know that a diplomat told him at a reception, "I've been in palaces all over the world, and I've never seen flowers as beautiful as they are at the White House." My staff and I were proud.

## Peonies Only Bloom in May

Mrs. Reagan had beautiful taste, certainly, and she wanted everything to be *perfect*. This meant, not surprisingly, that she could be quite particular.

She had two very specific favorite roses: the 'Kyria', a pretty, pale peach color, and the 'Sonia', a slightly darker shade of peach. Any old peach rose would not do; we had to have 'Kyria' and 'Sonia' roses specifically in stock in the flower shop at all times, in case she wanted to give them as a gift, and to use in the bud vases in her dressing room and sometimes for dinners and special events, too. They were part of the abundant arrangements when Prince Charles and Princess Diana visited the White House during the Reagan administration. The décor was soft, feminine, and incredibly pretty, with peach tablecloths, ficus trees covered in tiny white lights, and huge vermeil bowls filled with hundreds of roses each — 'Kyria', 'Sonia', and a special rose called the 'Lady Di', a pale peach similar to the 'Kyria'. For the Reagans' final state dinner, for Margaret Thatcher, we made topiaries of 'Kyria' roses and placed them on peach-colored linen tablecloths.

Mrs. Reagan did not like lavender or purple flowers (she mentioned one time that a purple orchid looked like an "old lady" flower), so for eight years, we didn't have them in the White House. If someone sent her a bouquet that contained anything lavender or purple, we usually removed those stems before we showed it to her, because we knew she wouldn't like it.

Occasionally, Mrs. Reagan would call me at home with an idea or a suggestion for improvement. There was no caller ID back then, so when I'd pick up, I'd be a little caught off-guard when I heard the White House operator say, "Please hold for Mrs. Reagan." I was always happy to take her call, of course, but I never knew what to expect, and I must admit I had to laugh at her (not for her to hear, of course) when one evening around 5:00, she called and said, "I just wanted to let you know that two of the roses on my dressing table are drooped over." As I said, she was a perfectionist. I may have rolled my eyes a bit, but I simply replied, "Yes, Mrs. Reagan, we'll take care of it right away." And I got in touch with someone at the White House and made sure those roses were replaced immediately.

For dinners, Mrs. Reagan requested either pastel or white flowers — and generally all white for the most formal dinners, because she thought that was the most elegant look of all. Dottie told me early on that for any event, Mrs. Reagan always wanted us to recheck the flowers within an hour of the guests arriving to make sure that not a leaf was drooping and not a blossom was out of place. Usually everything was fine, or we had to make only minor tweaks, but once, about twenty minutes before her dinner guests arrived, Mrs. Reagan said, "Nancy, I'd like the fireplace in the Yellow Oval Room [where guests had cocktails before dinner] to look a little more finished. Could you please fill it with fern plants?"

I was responsible for all cut-flower arrangements, but the National Park Service handled potted plants. They were gone for the day, though, so I dashed to the back elevator with a cart, took it up to the third floor, and ran up the stairs to the roof, hoping there would be some ferns left in the greenhouse, which sits on the roof on the north side, where it is not visible from the street. Luckily, when I opened the door, I immediately spotted a line of fern plants ready to go. I loaded seven of them onto my cart and took them back down to the second floor. Then I carried two at a time by hand into the Yellow Oval Room, keeping the cart outside so it wouldn't leave wheel marks in the carpeting, and arranged them in the fireplace just minutes before the first guest showed up.

Mrs. Reagan also adored peonies. Once I made a flower sample that she fell in love with, a simple bowl of more than fifty blush peonies — no foliage, just full-blown peonies. After that she frequently wanted to use that same peony arrangement for dinners, whether they were in season or not. At that time we couldn't get just any flower we wanted at any time of year, so I had to tell her, "I'm sorry, Mrs. Reagan, but peonies only bloom in May." It was one of the very few times that she didn't get exactly what she wanted. She understood, but soon she requested peonies out of season again. As she readily admits, she needed to be "gently reminded" — over and over — that no matter how much she loved peonies, they flowered just one month a year and simply weren't available. This became a standing joke between us and we would both laugh about it when she'd

THE WHITE HOUSE

Dear Nancy—

Thanks so much for your nice note— I was so sorry not to see you but I loved the peonies to my room! Your pillow sits in my bedroom where I am reminded every day that peonies bloom in May! I was so great to see everyone + be back here—lots of memories.

Fondly Nancy Reagan

Mrs. Reagan's note to me about her beloved peonies, sent to me after she made a return visit to the White House, almost twenty years after she had lived there.

ask for the flowers out of season. When the Reagans left the White House, I made her a needlepointed pillow that read, "Peonies Bloom in May." She sent me a note almost twenty years later that read, "Your pillow sits in my bedroom where I am reminded every day that peonies bloom in May!"

I learned just how much careful consideration she gave to arrangements for events after making a flower sample for her that included fresh strawberries. She chose that sample, and then later that night at about 9:00 my phone rang at home. The White House operator told me Mrs. Reagan was calling, and when she came on the line she said, "You know, I've been lying in bed thinking about this, and I don't want strawberries in the flowers after all." I assured her that I'd present her with new samples, without strawberries, the next day.

Mrs. Reagan knew exactly what she wanted, and basically that's the way things were supposed be done. But I never saw her be unkind to anyone about it — the only uncomfortable incident I remember was during the third year of President Reagan's second term when she called me in the flower shop and asked me to come up to her office on the second floor to see her. When I entered her office, she was irritably tapping a pen against her desk. "I am sick and tired," she said, "of finding dead flowers in this bathroom." (She was referring to the bathroom adjoining her office; it was the bathroom guests used, and indeed, one of my staff had forgotten to remove the flowers in there when the guests left, so there were several bud vases of very unattractive dead freesia.) "And furthermore," she added curtly, "the towels need to be changed." The flowers were completely our fault, so I apologized — and believe me, it never happened again. The towels, on the other hand, were not my responsibility, but I didn't mention that. I said, "Yes, ma'am, I'll let housekeeping know immediately." I did, and I'm fairly certain they never let dirty towels linger in the guest bathroom again.

I never knew Mrs. Reagan to be more particular than she was when we were getting ready for Mikhail Gorbachev and his wife to visit Washington in December 1987. Word came down to me from Mrs. Reagan through Ted Graber that every time the Gorbachevs came into a room, Mrs. Reagan wanted to have different flowers there. Ted said she really wanted to impress Mrs. Gorbachev — to knock her socks off. The centerpieces for the dinner were all white: white amaryllis and white freesia with a few white roses sprinkled in, on a white linen tablecloth. There were several other events for the Gorbachevs during their three-day visit, and, at Mrs. Reagan's request, we completely changed the flowers in the State Dining Room each day before they entered it.

## A Lighter Side

Yes, Mrs. Reagan was serious much of the time, and very interested in making sure things were perfect, but she could be lighthearted and joke around, too. She definitely showed a sense of humor at times, about herself as much as anything else. I think this aspect of her personality is often forgotten.

Early on, at the 1982 Gridiron Dinner, a white-tie event hosted by a small, private club of journalists, Mrs. Reagan got up on stage, in a costume of hideous-looking clothes, and sang these lyrics to the tune of the song "Second-Hand Rose": "I'm wearing second-hand clothes/ Second-hand clothes/ They're quite the style/ In the spring fashion shows/ Even my new trench coat with fur collar/ Ronnie bought for ten cents on the dollar." She cracked up the audience, got a standing ovation, and came back for an encore.

In response to a popular postcard featuring a composite photo of her wearing a crown, with the caption "Queen Nancy," Mrs. Reagan said to the crowd gathered at the 1981 Alfred E. Smith Memorial Dinner in New York City, "Now that's silly . . . I'd never wear a crown — it messes up your hair." And after the ruckus over the new White House china she ordered, she joked about a new charity organization she was starting: The Nancy Reagan Home for Wayward China.

Even when she was dealing with intensely personal difficulties, Mrs. Reagan employed her sense of humor. After President Reagan underwent surgery for colon cancer, I know she was deeply worried about him, but I think occasional moments of levity helped her cope. For example, immediately following the president's surgery, the White House was inundated with gifts of flowers. I brought a whole cartload of flowers to the second floor and set them on the dining room table. We placed one arrangement after another throughout the Residence, and we were running out of spots for them. I told Mrs. Reagan we had a few more and asked where she would like them. She put her hand to her forehead in mock exasperation and said, "Frankly, my dear, I don't give a damn!" We both laughed and I took the extra flowers back to the shop.

At Christmastime, when the decorations at the White House were subject to more scrutiny than ever, Mrs. Reagan was less interested in aesthetic perfection than she was in having fun and incorporating children into the season. She always wanted the theme to be related to children ("Mother Goose," which featured lots of sculpted geese with red scarves, popcorn strings, gingerbread men, and candy canes, and "Children's Christmas Songs" were two of her favorites). She also insisted that we use the ornaments made by teenagers from Second Genesis, a drug rehabilitation program, even when her interior designer vetoed them. Bill Hixson, the founder of the floral design school I attended, volunteered to help with decorations at the White House at Christmastime, and he told me that when Ted Graber saw the volunteers hanging handmade snowflakes, he shouted, "Get those snowflakes off the tree!" An hour later (we think after Mrs. Reagan got word of the removal of the ornaments), he returned and said, "Why don't you put those snowflakes back?" I always appreciated that, for her, supporting a cause near and dear to her heart (she famously championed the war on drugs) and making teenagers happy trumped taking things too seriously and having a perfectly polished tree.

President Reagan was happy and friendly, and he had a good sense of humor, too. I only saw him a few times a year, but whenever I did he had a smile on his face, even the time when I ran into him in the Residence as he was coming out of an exercise session in his gym shorts. "Well," he said with a twinkle in his eye, "I think one of us is in the wrong place." His genial remark put me at ease, and I didn't worry about it at all. Another time I was surprised to find him in the West Hall watching news programs on television when I went to check on the flowers fairly early on a Sunday morning. "Good morning!" he said. "How are you?" Startled, I blurted out, "Hello, Mr. President. I'm . . . just checking on my flowers." He replied with a smile, "Well, I'm just watching my shows!" We both had a laugh — and continued with what we were doing.

## A Difficult Year

As I got to know Mrs. Reagan and saw more of what went on behind the scenes, I started to realize that it must be very lonely sometimes to be the first lady. Despite all the events and parties, it's very difficult to socialize casually or to get out and about. She can't just say, "I'm going shopping now," and head out the door. She needs to go with an entourage, and someone calls ahead to the store to let them know, and no other shoppers can enter while she's there. It must be incredibly uncomfortable. She sometimes had friends, like Betsy Bloomingdale and even Frank Sinatra, come to the White House for lunch, and when they did it always put her in a great mood. I think it made her happy to have the company. But I don't think she had many close friends in Washington, and on many days she ate by herself, sitting with a TV tray in the West Hall. She also spent a great deal of

69

time talking on the phone, which was probably the easiest way for her to socialize, but I would imagine it didn't make up for the lack of face-to-face contact with her friends.

Mrs. Reagan always wanted to present a perfect image to guests of the White House, and so, as I mentioned earlier, she insisted that we do a last-minute check of the flowers soon before guests arrived for any event, whether it was a state dinner or a more intimate gathering in the private dining room on the second floor of the Residence. She was hosting just such a small dinner one night in early October 1987 — less than three months after the president had surgery to treat his colon cancer. Her guests were due at 7:00 p.m., and around 6:00, I was alone in the dining room making a few final tweaks, removing anything that had started to wilt and making sure each flower looked perfect. She suddenly walked into the room from the adjoining beauty salon. I don't think she was expecting anyone to be there. When she saw that it was me, without any warning or other greeting, she blurted out, "Nancy, I have breast cancer," and burst into tears. Her emotional admission got to me, and I started crying, too. "Oh, Mrs. Reagan, I am so sorry," I said, and we hugged. "It's going to be all right," she replied. We stood together for a few moments without saying anything, and then she wiped her tears away and said, "Well, I'm going to go get ready."

She had just learned about her diagnosis that afternoon, but she didn't cancel the dinner. After her brief outburst with me, she retreated to her bedroom and emerged less than an hour later, looking perfect, to greet her guests as graciously as she always did.

About two weeks later, she had a mastectomy at Bethesda Naval Hospital. The next morning, the president's personal assistant called and asked me to meet the president in the Lower Cross Hall on the ground floor of the White House. He wanted to bring her a bouquet of her favorite flowers, so of course I put together an arrangement of her beloved 'Kyria' roses. I remember feeling sad that the reason I was sending her these beautiful flowers was because she was dealing with cancer and its consequences. I was glad we had her favorites in stock, and I wanted it to be special. I wished I could do more to make her feel better, but I knew the flowers were the only thing I could do.

As I handed the president the flowers, I said, "Please send Mrs. Reagan my love. We're all thinking about her." He thanked me, and as he left the White House, he told the gathered press, "I've got a date with a girl in Bethesda." Soon after, President Reagan sent me a photo of the moment when I handed him the flowers. (The president's personal photographer, who travels with him almost everywhere, was with the president in the Lower Cross Hall when I gave him the flowers.) Written on the photo was a note that said, "To Nancy Clarke, who makes everything so beautiful. All best wishes, Ronald Reagan."

I didn't see President and Mrs. Reagan together very often, but I knew there was a lot of speculation that their relationship was something of an act that they put on. From what little my staff members and I did see, that wasn't the case. They seemed to be extremely close, and they really were always kissing, holding hands, and being loving with each other, even behind the scenes. One year at Christmastime, we hung a mistletoe ball in the foyer outside the president's elevator. I happened to be nearby when they returned from a weekend at Camp David right after the decorations had gone up, and I saw him take her in his arms and kiss her as soon as he saw the mistletoe. It wasn't a photo opportunity (there just happened to be a photographer there); it was a moment of genuine affection. She was very protective of him, and my impression is that he adored her and she adored him.

Shortly after Mrs. Reagan returned to the White House following her mastectomy, her mother died in Arizona. She called to talk to me about it, and I could hear in her voice how very saddened and drained she was. "Nancy, I know they're not in season," she said wearily, "but is there any way that we can get lilies of the valley at my mother's funeral?" She had told me many times that these were her mother's favorite flowers. "Mrs. Reagan," I said, "if they are anywhere, I will find them for you and you will have them." So I did the only thing I could do to help her — I tracked down lilies of the valley from one of my wholesalers and made sure that they were shipped to Arizona for the funeral.

Mrs. Reagan and I never talked about her breast cancer or her mother's death again, but after that fall, there was a new, unspoken bond between us — and when we were together at events during the rest of the Reagan administration, we often held hands for a moment, which we'd never done before. The first time it happened was at the staff Christmas party that year. When she spotted me she came right over, took my hand, and said, "Nancy, it's so good to see you." As we continued to hold hands, I said, "Oh, Mrs. Reagan it's so good to see you, too. You look lovely." We didn't say anything more, but it was a warm, lovely moment.

Many years later, when President Reagan died, Mrs. Reagan stayed at Blair House, the president's guesthouse across the street from the White House. I had peonies delivered to her from the Residence staff. On June 11, 2004, several of us who had been on the Residence staff when President Reagan was in office were invited over to see her before she went to the funeral service at the National Cathedral. It was a gray, cloudy day and a light rain had begun to fall, which seemed right for the sadness we were feeling that day. Mrs. Reagan made her way slowly down the steps of Blair House, dressed in a simple black suit with a gold necklace. She was pale and very thin, but her eyes shone bright. As she reached the bottom of the steps, she looked at me and said, "Thank you for my peonies." Tears filled her eyes, and mine. I was grateful that we could share this moment and that Mrs. Reagan's beloved peonies had stayed in bloom a little later that year, as if just for her.

# Compassionate Charm: Barbara Bush

*I love Nancy Clarke. Nancy is truly one of the most creative people I have ever met. I so enjoyed getting to know her and working with her during our years living in the White House. My first memory of Nancy was in February of 1989, right after we moved into the White House. Nancy asked me what I wanted the Christmas theme to be that year. I was shocked — that was ten and a half months away! By the time December rolled around, I understood just why she needed the notice. Each Christmas Nancy and her team (including many, many volunteers!) would decorate the White House in the most magical and magnificent ways. We felt like we were living in a winter wonderland!*

*Nancy had a way of making everything beautiful all year long. Our whole family loved Nancy, and I am glad we lived in the White House while she worked there. She was — and is — a brilliant, generous, talented, and kind lady and friend. So I will finish this where I started: I love Nancy Clarke.*

*— Barbara Bush*

**B**arbara Bush is known for her very quick wit — and for occasionally making outrageous comments. During the 1984 presidential campaign, she famously stated that she couldn't say what she thought of Geraldine Ferraro, "but it rhymes with rich." More recently, in late 2010, she said of Sarah Palin, "I think she's very happy in Alaska . . . and I hope she'll stay there."

Her personality isn't any different behind closed doors;

if anything, the comments I heard from her in private were even funnier and *more* pointed than those she makes publicly. Much of what she said surprised me. But she never said anything with malice. In fact, she was the kindest and most gracious first lady I ever worked with. She was simply natural and honest and very talkative, and she said whatever sprang into her mind. When giving my volunteers a tour of her private quarters, she pointed to an antique portrait on the wall and said, "Portrait painters always flatter their subjects. Can you imagine how ugly this lady really was?"

She was also practically unflappable. She rolled with everything that came her way and dealt calmly with almost every situation that I saw her in. Once, a member of the Residence staff was having a *really* bad day. This staff person had forgotten to take her medication, and she started throwing pillows around the Residence. Then she stormed in to where Mrs. Bush was watching the morning news in the beauty salon and snapped off the television. Mrs. Bush didn't get angry (not once in four years did I see her get angry); all she said was, "My, aren't we feeling our oats today!"

Another time, a volunteer named Laslo Sute, who was helping us with the Christmas decorations and who didn't speak English very well, happened to be in the Blue Room placing ornaments on the tree when Mrs. Bush walked in with her beloved dog (and frequent sidekick), Millie. He looked down from his ladder and asked, "Is that the bitch?" Pointing to her dog, Mrs. Bush said, "Who, her? Or me?" Everyone in the room was silent for a moment, and then all of us — including Mrs. Bush — broke out laughing.

She saw the humor in everything — including the idea

that, as a first lady, she was a fashion role model. "I mean, look at me," she said to the press soon after President Bush took office. "My mail tells me a lot of fat, white-haired, wrinkled ladies are tickled pink!"

The Residence staff had a sense before the Bushes moved into the White House that Mrs. Bush would be fun to work with. Because George H.W. Bush had served as the vice president for eight years under President Reagan, everyone on our staff was familiar with him and Mrs. Bush before they became the first family.

The Bushes had visited the White House many times to attend events and, like every vice president, George Bush had an office in the West Wing. We kept fresh flowers in his office, so we often saw him when we delivered them. He always said "hello" or "thank you" and occasionally asked what kind of flowers we were using that day. "Good morning!" I remember him saying to me one day. "Those flowers are even prettier than the ones you brought last week." He was friendly (like Mrs. Bush), but he tended to be soft-spoken, in contrast to his candid wife.

At Christmastime, we decorated the vice president's West Wing office with a Christmas tree and sent a holiday topiary to his home at Number One Observatory Circle. Mrs. Bush always sent a lovely thank-you note after the topiary arrived and told us where she was using it that year and how well it coordinated with her decorations. "This is such a happy sharing time of the year, and I am so grateful to you all for sharing with us," she wrote in 1985. "A very Merry Christmas to each and every one of you, and a well and happy 1986."

I had met Mrs. Bush several times when she and the vice president showed up early for White House dinners during the Reagan administration, when they were part of the official welcoming party. They would often peek into the dining room as we were putting the finishing touches on the table decorations or floral arrangements. She usually told me how much she liked the flowers we were using that night or commented about a certain shade of rose or some unusual variety. "Those peach roses open so well," she observed before one dinner.

One night Vice President and Mrs. Bush came in as we were lighting the votive candles on all the tables before the guests entered the dining room. Mrs. Reagan liked freesia sticking out from the sides and tops of floral arrangements, and for this dinner I had the freesia so far out that it almost touched the glassware. As the candles we were lighting started really burning, many of the freesia tips caught on fire. This didn't happen on just one table; nearly all of the tables seemed to light up at once. My staff and I raced around trying to put out the little fires when both the vice president, in his tuxedo, and Mrs. Bush, in her gown, jumped right in to help us. They moved the candles out of the way and pulled out the burning freesia, shaking them and blowing on them to stop the burning. Once all the flames were finally out and the smoke was almost gone (fresh flowers do smoke when burned), we all laughed.

On President Bush's Inauguration Day, as always, the Residence staff worked frantically to get the new first family moved in. Once their furniture and clothes were in place and things had gotten to the point where we were starting to take flower arrangements up to the second floor, my staff and I got off the back elevator and I led the way into the dining room, which leads to the West Hall, so we could distribute the flowers to the many different rooms. Barbara

Bush happened to be standing in the dining room when I came through the doors. I was cutting through the dining room as I always did on my way to placing flowers in the Residence. She looked at me and said, for no apparent reason, "Nancy, you are a first lady's dream come true." Of course, Ronn Payne, a designer on my staff who was constantly joking around, teased me about the comment later. "You're a dream!" he told me repeatedly over the course of the next few days. But I knew we were getting off on the right foot with Mrs. Bush from day one.

And that remained true throughout the Bush administration. The whole time we were there, I felt like we couldn't do anything wrong. That's a nice feeling to have. Truly, not once in four years did we disagree about a floral arrangement. It was different from working with Mrs. Reagan, who was so particular and had specific ideas about exactly how things should be. Whereas Mrs. Bush told me not to worry if an arrangement dropped a few blossoms on the table during dinner ("It's first impressions that count," she said), with Mrs. Reagan we'd had to use a soft brush to remove any pollen that fell on the petals of white lilies — she insisted on lilies with stamens still attached because she thought they looked more natural. Keeping them pollen-free was a nightmare.

Mrs. Bush just had an easygoing personality. I felt she was delighted to be living at the White House, loved everything about the place, and appreciated everyone around her. She was less formal and more familiar with our staff than other first ladies. Normally, when a first lady had a guest visiting in the West Hall, anyone on the Residence staff who was working on the second floor would step out of sight or come back later to finish their work when the guests were gone. When Mrs. Bush was there, however, if she saw one of us she immediately called us in to be introduced to her guests and talked about what we did at the White House. When the president's sister visited the Bushes at the White House, I happened to walk into the West Hall when she and Mrs. Bush were there. Mrs. Bush said to me, "Nancy, I would like you to meet Nancy Ellis. She's George's sister." When I heard her first name, I smiled and said, "It's so nice to meet you. We certainly have a great first name, don't we?" And the three of us giggled about it. Mrs. Bush made us feel like we were friends rather than staff.

## Easygoing Style
Soon after the inauguration, Mrs. Bush told me during my very first visit with her in the Residence that she thought the existing furnishings on the second floor were lovely and that Mrs. Reagan had done a beautiful job of redecorating. She also told me the style of flower arrangements we'd been doing for Mrs. Reagan was perfect and to leave everything as it was. And often, when we thought it was time to replace an arrangement because a few blooms were on their way out, she'd insist, "Oh, they're fine for a couple more days!"

The only room Mrs. Bush wanted to change was the family room, located just off the bedroom she shared with the president, so it would coordinate with a needlepoint rug she'd made and had brought with her. It was a beautiful rug with a pale bluish-green background. Centered in the middle were flowers that spread out to the edges in shades of pink, rose, cream, white, and green. When her interior decorator completed the room, he coordinated the colors of the rug with a chintz fabric for draperies and matching

The doctors are in! Dottie Temple (left), chief floral designer from 1981 to 1985, and I had fun injecting water lilies with muscle relaxant to keep them open for the state dinner on May 7, 1981, honoring Japanese Prime Minister Zenko Suzuki.

Movie star Gene Kelly (second from left) and Beverly Sills, America's "Queen of Opera" (far right), gather with President and Mrs. Reagan around a regal white centerpiece in the Blue Room in May 1982.

In May 1983, then-Vice President George H. W. Bush paid a rare visit
to the flower shop. He said he wanted to see where we actually worked,
after having watched us change the flowers in his office twice a week.

Teddy bears played an
adorable role in our
Christmas decorations
in 1983.

In May 1984, Michael Jackson visited the White House and received an award from the Reagan administration for his support of the National Campaign Against Teenage Drunk Driving.

President and Mrs. Reagan pose for a formal photo with me near the end of President Reagan's first term, in 1984. It is a lovely White House tradition for the president and first lady to take a photograph once every administration with each member of their official staff.

Mrs. Reagan didn't come to the flower shop very often, but on this particular occasion she stopped by to speak with me about the centerpieces for an upcoming dinner while a film crew recorded her visit.

Mrs. Reagan loved red china and gorgeous peonies, and one of her favorite centerpieces ever was the arrangement of peonies seen here in the State Dining Room for a dinner for Prime Minister Rajiv Gandhi of India in June 1985.

The State Dining Room is all aglow and ready for guests of honor Prince Charles and Princess Diana, who visited the White House in November 1985. Ted Graber, Mrs. Reagan's interior decorator, designed this dinner.

Guests at the November 1985 dinner for Prince Charles and Princess Diana didn't realize that we had used chicken wire to reinforce the centerpieces — it was necessary in order to hold more than 150 roses (per arrangement!) in place.

For the party after the November 1985 dinner for Prince Charles and Princess Diana, who's seen here dancing with John Travolta, I filled huge vermeil bowls with hundreds of roses each.

I didn't work only with flowers and table settings: For a Christmas display in 1985, I painted faces of children on fabric and then attached them to the dolls seen here. My staff and I also made the clothing for these figures, which were up to two-and-a-half feet tall.

In December 1985, I got a warm hug from Larry Hagman, who took a break from playing J. R. Ewing on *Dallas* to don a Santa suit.

For the state dinner for President León Febres Cordero of Ecuador in January 1986, we used two of Mrs. Reagan's favorite colors — peach and red — for the tablecloth and floral arrangements.

Here Mrs. Reagan and I are going over details of the centerpieces for the state dinner for Cameroon President Paul Biya, February 28, 1986.

Strings of bee lights gave the Rose Garden an ethereal look for the outdoor state dinner for President José Sarney of Brazil in September 1986. These enchanting decorations came together thanks to the combined efforts of Mrs. Reagan's interior decorator, Ted Graber; the White House floral staff; and the National Park Service.

In October 1987, when President Reagan asked for a bouquet of flowers to bring to Mrs. Reagan, who was in the hospital recovering from breast cancer surgery, I gave him an arrangement of the 'Kyria' roses she liked so much.

To Nancy Clarke - Who makes the place so pretty. Every good wish & Best Regards. Ronald Reagan

Here we are in December 1987 doing our annual Christmas walk-through. I am showing President Reagan (back, right) and Mrs. Reagan (front, right) the decorations in the Green Room. Accompanying us are Mrs. Reagan's interior decorator, Ted Graber (left), and Chief Usher Gary Walters (back left).

Here I am with President Reagan in December 1987, reviewing the White House Christmas decorations. Notice that the president isn't the only one in pants! (Until Hillary Clinton became first lady, my female staff and I weren't allowed to wear pants unless we were setting up the holiday decorations.)

President and Mrs. Reagan were often playful and loving in front of the White House staff. Here they share a kiss under the mistletoe after viewing the holiday decorations in December 1987.

Mrs. Reagan, with the hilarious Dom DeLuise as Santa, hosted the press in the Blue Room in December 1987.

In December 1987, the National Park Service decorated the East Garden Room in the East Wing with "dazzlers," which are Christmas trees constructed of white and peach poinsettias.

For the December 1987 state dinner for Mikhail Gorbachev, General Secretary of the Soviet Union, and his wife, Raisa, we used the Reagan china and created centerpieces made of white amaryllis and white freesia. We were given word that Mrs. Reagan wanted new flowers installed every day to impress the Gorbachevs.

President Reagan offers up a toast to General Secretary Gorbachev in the State Dining Room in December 1987. Mrs. Reagan loved white flowers, so we created all-white arrangements for the tables and the mantelpieces.

In the flower shop in June 1989, First Lady Barbara Bush and I discuss a centerpiece of red roses and beautiful lilies for a dinner honoring Prime Minister Robert J. L. Hawke of Australia.

Fireworks displays above the White House were spectacular.

Mrs. Barbara Bush liked unusual centerpieces, so we included Cybis porcelain figurines with the pink floral arrangements for the dinner to honor President Corazon C. Aquino of the Philippines in November 1989.

By the time President and Mrs. Bush visited with me and the volunteers in the Cross Hall as we decorated for Christmas in 1989, I was already covered in fake snow.

This is a peek at what the Second Floor Dining Room looks like in the private residence when set for a private dinner, April 1989. Note the outdoors-inspired, hand-blocked wallpaper mural.

When I decorated the private residence, I always took the first family's personal taste into account. For President and Mrs. Bush we hung traditional wreaths, according to their preferences, in the windows of the Second Floor Dining Room for Christmas 1990.

upholstered furniture. We generally put pretty pink and cream lilies or cream or peach amaryllis in that room, which had a warm, comfortable feeling. Every time I went in, I felt like I could plop down in one of the chairs and be right at home. (No, I never did!)

The rest of the second floor remained much as it was during the Reagan administration — and so did the flowers, except that with Mrs. Bush we were free to use lavender and purple flowers, which she enjoyed, but which had been off-limits while Mrs. Reagan was in the White House.

In terms of personal style, Mrs. Bush was relatively conservative. She wore simple suits and tailored dresses, often in shades of blue. For formal events, she wore silk taffeta gowns, often with long sleeves and fuller skirts. She almost always wore her signature triple strand of pearls. (One of my Christmas volunteers, Gladys Leonard, was an older woman with snow-white hair and blue eyes, who loved to wear blue as much as Mrs. Bush did. Mrs. Bush called her "my little sister" and once gave her a triple string of faux pearls, which Gladys treasured. When we traveled in the White House van, as we came out the gate to the White House, Gladys would sit in the back of the van with her white hair and her pearls and wave to the tourists. Of course, the tourists thought they were seeing Mrs. Bush and would wave back and cheer. We thought it was hilarious. When Gladys died, her family placed those beloved pearls from Mrs. Bush around her neck.) I don't recall seeing Mrs. Bush wear pants very often, except in pictures taken at the Bushes' Kennebunkport home — and when she was coming or going from exercising.

Mrs. Bush liked to wear Keds tennis shoes to and from her workouts. She liked them so much that once the president ordered an assortment of about twenty pairs of them for her birthday. They were stored in the paint shop next to our office until her birthday, so Wendy, one of my designers, and I went in to see all the colors. I thought it was a fun and thoughtful gift from the president. Some were striped, some were printed with designs, some were in pastel colors, and there were many in shades of blue. Once she came into our office in the morning wearing two shoes from completely different pairs, and of course we laughed about it with her.

Mrs. Bush occasionally stopped by the flower shop first thing in the morning wearing her tennis clothes after playing tennis with her friends on the South Grounds. Other times she'd be dressed in a jogging suit or even a robe, with wet hair, after swimming in the pool near the Oval Office. The first time she "popped in," we were all quite surprised, as we almost never saw a first lady dressed so informally off the second floor. But it became routine and we loved to see her, because she always seemed genuinely interested in learning about whatever we were creating that day.

Mrs. Bush liked almost every type of flower. She gardened herself in Kennebunkport and could name many varieties I had never worked with. In arrangements we made for her, we used a lot of mixed varieties and colors and she always told us they were perfect. She also enjoyed using *objets d'art* mixed in with the flowers, because she said that gave guests who didn't know each other a topic of conversation. We used sculpted porcelain figures for a Philippines State Dinner, needlepoint houses for a ladies' luncheon, and needlepoint ornaments for a luncheon for Senate spouses. One Christmas, when the entire Bush family went to Camp David for the holidays, I sent them centerpieces that were made from Steiff teddy bears that we had in storage (we'd used them during a Nancy Reagan Christmas) and carnations. When New Year's had passed and my containers and bears had not been returned, I called Camp David, and (much to my horror, because those bears were so expensive) they told me Mrs. Bush had given them to the staff to take home to give to their families. It was a lovely gesture on her part, but I should have let the Camp David staff know we needed to have them back!

At the beginning of the administration, before a luncheon or dinner, I would show Mrs. Bush several sample setups (complete with flowers, china, flatware, glassware, and tablecloths) that her social secretary, Laurie Firestone, had approved. But she had attended many state dinners during the Reagan administrations and was very familiar with the table setups and available china patterns. So after a while, we did away with some of the formal sample previews, and often I would just show her a few loose flowers and the tablecloth while she worked in her office. She had set up her office in the beauty salon, which had great views of the North Grounds and Pennsylvania Avenue. Most of the first ladies loved that beauty salon — it was strictly their domain — and most had a desk area in there, too. When I came upstairs to change flowers or talk about ideas for an event, if I didn't see Mrs. Bush immediately, I would call out "yoo-hoo," and soon I would hear "yoo-hoo" back from wherever she was. For four years, that was how I found her when I was looking for her on the second or third floor.

Mrs. Bush almost always wanted to use the Johnson china, which had a soft ivory background. Each dinner plate featured a gold eagle surrounded by a band of American wildflowers, and each of the dessert plates had a single state flower in the center — there was a plate to represent each of the fifty states. She used this china for almost every event she held. She told me several times that she thought Mrs. Johnson had made a beautiful choice in selecting the pattern.

## Loyal Companion

The Bushes moved into the White House with a springer spaniel named Millie, who was an important part of Mrs. Bush's life and traveled everywhere with her. Mrs. Bush always took Millie with her to visit children's groups. When she visited our shop, Millie was always at her side. She was never bothered by strangers and I never heard her bark or growl at anyone. She seemed mellow and relaxed wherever she was taken; she immediately made herself at home and would just lie down somewhere.

When Millie was about to deliver puppies, the chief usher placed a wooden box in the center of the floor of the beauty salon (not far from Mrs. Bush's desk). Millie delivered her puppies there and stayed there to take care of them. Mrs. Bush wrote a book called *Millie's Book* (published in 1992) that described life in the White House and the presidency from her dog's perspective. It was filled with photos and personal observations of happenings at the White House that only Mrs. Bush could make, and it became a best-seller. She donated all proceeds from the book to the Barbara Bush Foundation for Family Literacy; children's literacy was a favorite cause of hers.

Mrs. Bush had Millie photographed in almost every room in the White House for the book. They were even photographed sitting together at a table in the State Dining Room — when it was set up for a state dinner in honor of the prime minister of Australia! (A few members of the staff questioned whether that was appropriate, but it was just Mrs. Bush's style to be casual about such things.) Millie was even a "guest" at some events — there's another picture of her in the book, sitting behind Mrs. Bush at a dinner for cabinet officials in the Rose Garden.

## Holiday Cheer

Well before the Bushes' first Christmas in the White House, Gary Walters, the chief usher, and I went to see Mrs. Bush to talk about what she wanted to do for decorations. It was only February, just a few weeks after she'd moved in, and she was surprised we were there so early in the year to talk about the holidays. But when we explained to her the extent of the decorating process, she began to understand why we needed so many months. Before we started talking to the first lady about themes, my staff and I met with the chief usher for a brainstorming meeting. Then we presented the first lady

A note from Mrs. Barbara Bush about her idea for a needlepoint tree as the Christmas decoration theme for 1991.

with a list of ideas for consideration, from which she would choose. Whatever we devised as the main theme for the Blue Room tree would be carried over to decorations for the rest of the White House. Because Mrs. Bush was such an avid supporter of children's literacy, in 1989 one idea we presented was that the Blue Room tree could contain ornaments representing such favorite characters from children's literature as the lion, the tin man, and the scarecrow from *The Wonderful Wizard of Oz*. She loved the idea as soon as we mentioned it, and she suggested that instead of a tree skirt, we should place stacks of children's books around the base of the tree.

Once those decorations were in place and the parties were well under way, she asked me what we might do the following year. She had realized over the course of our preparations how much advance planning was really required. I came up with a list of theme options, one of which was "A Needlework Christmas." I knew she was an enthusiastic needlepointer, and I wasn't surprised when she chose that one.

We developed the idea of making three-dimensional needlepoint ornaments, and agreed that we should push this idea back until two years in the future, because we both knew how long a single needlepoint project takes to complete — and we were going to need a lot of them. At the time, I never dreamed I would be the one creating the three-dimensional designs, as I just assumed an outside organization would take care of it. Mrs. Bush wanted the Saintly Stitchers, a needlepoint group from her church in Texas, to be involved, and she also wanted us to reach out to the different White House staffs (or their families) who needlepointed to help us. She asked me to make a Raggedy

Ann figure for her to needlepoint as a sample of the type of ornaments we would create for the tree.

She didn't know this, but when my husband was in Vietnam and my children and I went back to Illinois to live with my family, I took up needlepointing to keep busy, and I actually won third place in the local fair. But making a three-dimensional Raggedy Ann design was harder than I thought it would be. I bought canvas and drew the front, and then I tried to count stitches to make the back match up, but it didn't work very well. Every day, Mrs. Bush would call to see if her pattern was ready, and of course, I had to say, "No, not quite yet." I struggled with more canvas, more drawings, and more phone calls from Mrs. Bush, but finally I got it close enough to give to her. In the days that followed, I saw the pattern lying around on an ottoman or sofa with partially completed orange curly hair, and then a little face, and then a blue dress, until Mrs. Bush had completed one side and then started the back side.

By then it was early spring, and she asked Lida Browder, the president of the Saintly Stitchers, to come for a visit. Both Lida and I were asked to the second floor to talk about the project. On Mrs. Bush's lap was the Raggedy Ann canvas that I had made. She flipped it over to Lida and asked, "Does she know what she's doing?" Lida studied it closely and replied, "Yes, she does." Well, that was it; I was off on a project that I still hadn't quite figured out yet. (After much trial and error, though, I did finally devise a solution using graph paper, and I created a perfect system for creating three-dimensional needlepoint patterns!)

Once we knew how to do it right, my staff and I designed patterns for needlepoint ornaments of everything we could think of, from fruits to stars to ballerinas to stockings, and even a mermaid. The project grew larger and larger as staff members stopped by our shop to pick up a pattern for their mother or sister. Eventually we took over the office next to mine and turned it into a "needlepoint shop" with skeins of yarn and patterns. We were happily surprised that many men who worked in the White House (who had never stitched anything in their lives) contributed to our needlepoint efforts. When the completed ornaments started to come in from both the Saintly Stitchers and the staff members and their relatives, Mrs. Bush stopped by our shop every few days to see what else had arrived.

Christmas that year was a tremendous success and many articles about it appeared in needlepoint and women's magazines. My Raggedy Ann and Raggedy Andy patterns and photographs of the completed needlepoint figures appeared in *Ladies' Home Journal* in December 1991. The article stated, "Mrs. Bush hopes you'll make copies of these treasures for your own tree and share this new White House tradition of decorating with needlepoint." (What's more, kits of my two patterns, complete with yarn, were sold for years in the George Bush Library museum shop.) When Mrs. Bush saw all the colorful needlepoint figures — including the Millie she had made herself — decorating the 18-foot tree, she looked quite proud and told reporters, "We just didn't realize it would all turn out to be so grand."

## A Gracious Lady

In so many situations, Mrs. Bush had a personal quality that impressed me greatly — her gracious thoughtfulness. It just came naturally to her. One day, at Christmastime, she called me over to look at the pin she was wearing.

She often showed me gifts she had received, and this was a handmade gift from someone in the Midwest. Oh my, I thought to myself, that's really not very pretty. It was a metallic Christmas tree pin that had an odd combination of colors and was not particularly well made. Mrs. Bush acknowledged that she'd seen prettier pins. "But, Nancy," she said, "I'm wearing it anyway, because if someone could take so much time to make it for me, I feel the least I can do is wear it." I often think back to her comment when I receive something I don't care for or a gift I don't like. I go ahead and wear it or use it anyway, following Mrs. Bush's example.

She showed the same consideration, whether dealing with volunteers, the staff, or royalty. I recall one particular instance when a queen was scheduled to come visit her at the White House. All of a sudden, the queen showed up unexpectedly early, while Mrs. Bush was still in the beauty salon getting her hair done. Without hesitation, she got up (her hair was all teased and in disarray) and greeted the queen. She would not keep a queen waiting, no matter what her own hair looked like.

Each year, when all the Christmas decorating was completed and the volunteers had returned home, I used to stand next to her (at her desk in the salon) with a stack of thank-you letters that would be sent to volunteers who had helped during the holidays. I would tell her about each one individually and then she would write a personalized note on the bottom of each person's letter. No other first lady did anything like this. She always took the time to be gracious to everyone and my volunteers adored her.

More than any other president I worked for, President Bush had a way of inviting people over at the last minute for private dinners. Mrs. Bush warned me that he had been doing this for years and told me to use whatever flowers we had on hand and not to buy anything special. I heard she told the kitchen to fix anything they happened to have available, too. I always made sure we kept a few basic flowers ready for occasions just like this. Such planning ahead came in handy especially when we were about to leave for the day and we'd get a phone call from the ushers' office to let us know that "we'll be having ten for dinner tonight." I would scramble to put together an arrangement from whatever was in the refrigerator that day. And (thank goodness!) Mrs. Bush always liked it.

In addition to last-minute dinner guests, we had plenty of official and state dinners, too. Prior to those, Mrs. Bush occasionally called to ask me to come upstairs to go through the gowns in her closet to see if I might be able to match flowers and tablecloths with one of them. She certainly liked matching colors, as I saw when she redecorated the family room with matching draperies and a matching sofa and chairs, but it seemed a little unusual for a dinner — but she wasn't being high-maintenance, just having fun. Mrs. Reagan and Laura Bush occasionally asked me to make sure that the flowers in the background of their television tapings or photographs were coordinated with their clothes, but Barbara Bush was the only first lady whose closet I ever looked through.

In May 1991, Queen Elizabeth came to visit the White House. Before I had even started thinking about the centerpieces for the state dinner in the queen's honor, Mrs. Bush called to let me know that she was going to wear a white lace-topped gown with a dark lavender skirt, and she wanted to use white peonies with a silvery purple rose she liked, called 'Purple Passion', for the centerpieces. I took samples of the rose and the peony to show her with a white tablecloth, and she said they would be a perfect match for her dress. After we made the centerpieces though, I realized they looked a little bland, so I spoke to Laurie Firestone, Mrs. Bush's social secretary, about it, and we added pink roses to her combination. The next day, Mrs. Bush told me that she was "surprised" to see the roses but nevertheless, she thought the centerpieces looked beautiful. I had never before changed a centerpiece for a first lady without checking with her first, and I probably shouldn't have — but luckily she liked it. Still, I never did that again!

When Operation Desert Storm was officially announced in January 1991 (when U.S. troops were sent to Kuwait), Mrs. Bush and Gary Walters happened to be visiting our shop. We had the television on when the announcement came over the news, and she said, "Oh, no. George has to send our boys to war." She often referred to our troops as "her boys" and frequently mentioned over the next few months how worried she was about them.

## A Few More Celebrations

During the last summer that the Bushes were in the White House, Mrs. Bush asked me to help their daughter, Dorothy (whom everyone calls Doro), with her wedding, which was going to be at Camp David in late June. Laurie and I planned the centerpieces (blush peonies and peach gerbera and roses on a mirrored plateau), chose tablecloths for the reception (peach cloths with white lace overlays), and flowers for the church (white peonies and snapdragons). Wendy Elsasser and Dianne Barbour, designers who worked with me at that time in the flower shop, helped me get everything ready at the White House, and then we loaded the flowers into the flower shop van. To be on the safe side, we made two bridal bouquets on the day before the wedding (soft peach roses and miniature white orchids), and I kept them in my refrigerator at home that night.

The next morning we headed to Camp David in Maryland, about an hour and half drive from the White House. I had never been to Camp David before, as it is the first family's private retreat and members of the Residence staff usually did not go there. Officially Camp David is a naval support facility and has its own navy staff. Generally, we just supported Camp David (or wherever the president was traveling) from the White House by sending up supplies and flowers. The only time we actually traveled with the president was when he attended the G7 or G8 Summits held in the United States every seven years. (I went with President Reagan to Williamsburg in 1983; with President Bush to Houston in 1990 — where I had the honor of escorting the prime minister of Japan and the chancellor of Germany through Houston's Museum of Fine Arts before a dinner that was held there; and with President Clinton to Denver in 1997.)

Once you arrive at the Camp, you can't drive your vehicle. Instead, everyone gets around in golf carts. Wendy, Dianne, and I got out of our van and saw Mrs. Bush coming down the road, driving a golf cart, with her white hair blowing in the wind. She pulled up and said, "Get in!" And off we went down a little path to see the chapel and the reception site. Along the path we saw small guest cabins sprinkled throughout the woods. Members of the military drove our van to "Aspen," the large cabin where the president and first lady stayed when they were at Camp David. The reception was going to be held on the slate patio behind the house, where tables were set up overlooking a pool. We worked out of the van on tables in the grass and in the Aspen kitchen. The interior of Aspen was rustic, with rough walls, a stone fireplace, and colorful upholstered furniture.

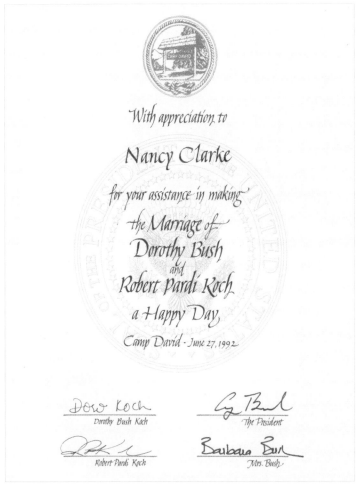

With appreciation to

Nancy Clarke

for your assistance in making

the Marriage of
Dorothy Bush
and
Robert Pardi Koch

a Happy Day,

Camp David - June 27, 1992

*Dorothy Bush Koch*

*The President*

*Robert Pardi Koch*

*Mrs. Bush*

A card from President George H.W. Bush and Mrs. Bush thanking me for helping with their daughter Dorothy's wedding at Camp David, June 27, 1992.

We took two large arrangements of white peonies and snapdragons to the chapel to place them on the altar. The chapel was simple and more contemporary than other buildings at Camp David, with an A-frame roof and wood paneling on the interior walls.

We then returned to Aspen to set up the reception dinner tables with cloths, overlays, and flowers. When everything was finished, we had a few minutes before the wedding, so I walked out to the front of Aspen and crossed the little road to a small pond. It was a beautiful summer day and the sun glimmered on the water. As I was standing there, watching the goldfish dart around in the shallow pond, President Bush — dressed in his suit for the wedding — walked up to me.

"Hi Nancy," he said. "I see you've found our goldfish. Do you see how large some of them have grown? They've been part of this pond for years."

I could sense how fond the president was of this place, which was so much quieter and more relaxed than the hustle and bustle of life in the White House. We spoke for a few more minutes, which was rare and exciting for me, because the president didn't usually have time to chat.

A few moments later, Wendy, Dianne, and I slipped into the back pews and watched the simple, lovely ceremony. When the bride and groom knelt at the altar, we saw that someone had put "Bush/Quayle 92" stickers on the soles of the groom's shoes. Everyone chuckled, but as far as I know, no one ever took credit for doing it.

By September of that year, the election polls didn't look good for the president — and of course he lost the election to Bill Clinton. Just after the election, it was time for us to begin decorating for Christmas. This was usually the time of year when everyone seemed to have the most fun, but not that year. It felt like we just had a job to do and we had to get through it, and I was sad because I so enjoyed working for the Bushes and knew it would be coming to an end shortly.

Even so, Mrs. Bush and the president came down to see what everyone was doing while we were decorating. They were there when we "snowed" the trees in the main Cross Hall with shredded Styrofoam, which we did the last night before the press preview and the beginning of all the parties. Deep piles of snow accumulated all over the floor. Suddenly, as if we couldn't let this Christmas come upon us without getting into the spirit of the holidays, we started joking and playing with the shredded Styrofoam. Gary Walters dumped a full box of it on my head and soon the volunteers were all throwing snow too. Everyone was laughing as the snow stuck in our hair or on our clothes and even got in our shoes. The volunteers were very careful about throwing snow when the president was near, but I noticed that even he had a few flakes on his clothes. The fun with the snow and the visit from the Bushes were wonderful for the volunteers, who had worked so hard to pull the decorations together.

We were all talking about how beautiful everything looked and telling Mrs. Bush about who had done exactly what. She posed for photographs and visited with everyone, but I could tell that her heart wasn't in this, her last Christmas at the White House. The spark was gone and she stayed for a shorter time than she had in previous years. After all the boisterous fun had subsided, I noticed that Mrs. Bush looked more pensive than usual. I couldn't help but wonder if she was thinking about how much she'd miss all the fun of these Christmas celebrations in the White House. Several volunteers, who had worked with us for many years, recognized the change, too, and mentioned to me that this year she seemed much quieter and visited less often.

Christmas seemed to come and go quickly that year, and suddenly it was the middle of January and we were seeing new faces from the transition teams visiting their new offices. Before the Bushes left the White House, Mrs. Bush turned the two front bedrooms on the second floor (next to the beauty shop) into a gift area for the staff. We each drew a number and then went in order to select two gifts. When my turn came, I was shocked to see the high quality of the gifts — dresses, jewelry, camera equipment, and so much more. These were both gifts she'd received over the years and personal items she wouldn't be taking with her when she left the White House. I selected a burgundy handbag — Chanel! — with a gold chain handle for myself and a set of camera lenses for my husband.

The day before Mrs. Bush left the White House, I went up to her office, which was still in the beauty salon. I didn't need to call out "yoo-hoo" one last time, for I found her just standing, gazing out the window, looking subdued in the morning light. I had seen her standing here so many times before, taking in the view of Pennsylvania Avenue and the White House gate. Her laptop used to be set up near this window, which she told me she had enjoyed so much over the years. She loved observing all that was going on below.

"Mrs. Bush," I said, trying to keep my emotions in check, "I've come to say good-bye."

She turned around and we both teared up and gave each other a long hug.

"Thank you so much," I said, "for allowing me to work for you."

She replied, "Oh, no, Nancy, thank you."

I remembered the laughs we'd had together — and how I knew her taste so well that I could show her just a few flowers and get a quick "Yes" — and the glittering Christmases we shared in the Blue Room, the majestic tree bedecked with needlepointed characters, including the Raggedy Ann and Raggedy Andy we had made the year before. And I recalled the times we spoke in this beauty salon, the first lady at her desk and Millie sitting happily by her side. We had shared so much in the past four years, and I couldn't bring myself to say good-bye.

# A Woman of Strength: Hillary Clinton

*I love the flowers and you!*
— *Hillary Clinton*

**B**efore I met Hillary Clinton for the first time, I was more intimidated and nervous than I'd ever been prior to meeting a first lady. Mrs. Clinton was a hard-hitting, high-powered attorney, and before the new first family moved in, there were rumors swirling around about how tough she was going to be while overseeing the White House. She was the first first lady to have an office in the West Wing and to have an official role as a presidential advisor, and she was rarely in the Residence during the first few months of the administration, at least when I was working there.

More than a week after she'd moved into the White House, I still hadn't seen her in person, and I'd received zero feedback from her about the flowers we were using to decorate the Residence. This worried me. President Clinton had promised during his campaign to eliminate twenty-five percent of the White House staff, and I was concerned for our team of five floral designers. All of this added up to a case of severe anxiety in the moments before my first encounter with Mrs. Clinton, while I waited in the State Dining Room for her to come in to look at flower samples for her first Governors' Dinner as first lady.

As she strode into the room with her social secretary and personal assistant in tow, I was quite literally holding my breath. It turned out there was no reason at all to be concerned. She walked right over to me with a wide grin on her face. I extended my hand to shake hers and said, "Hi Mrs. Clinton. I'm Nancy Clarke, and I'm the White House florist. We're so happy to have you here."

"Thank you," she said, still smiling, and then asked, "Well, what do we have here?" I breathed a sigh of relief. She emanated warmth and I liked her immediately.

She was direct and decisive, pointing immediately to the sample she liked best — a mix of hot pink, red, and white tulips — but saying she'd like it better if it were a little softer.

"I could add some phlox," I suggested, showing her some stems of pretty white blossoms.

"That would be perfect," she replied. She was right — it looked better that way. And that's how it was with her. She was honest, and I always knew where I stood, and we worked together quickly and efficiently. Though she could be distracted at times (not surprising, given how busy she was and all that went on during her White House years), she never let that interfere with our relationship, or the way she treated my staff or me.

Just before that first Governors' Dinner, Mrs. Clinton told the *New York Times* she was enjoying getting ready for the event. "I think it's fun," she said of all the preparations. I was surprised and happy that she seemed to be so engaged in the planning. I had wondered if she would be involved at all, given her West Wing obligations. For the rest of the administration, she was involved in selecting the flowers for every major dinner and luncheon.

## Questions of Taste

It's easy for me to describe the personal taste and style of most of the first ladies I worked for: Mrs. Reagan was elegant and sophisticated. Barbara Bush was conservative and traditional. Laura Bush loved clean, simple lines and monochromatic tones. Mrs. Clinton, on the other hand, was impossible to pin down — in terms of her clothes, her home-decorating style, even the way she wore her hair. She changed hairstyles more often than anyone I've ever met!

There were days when she looked fantastic, wearing a simple, elegant, well-tailored suit with her hair beautifully coiffed, tasteful jewelry, and subtle makeup. And then there were days she was much more playful with her clothing, and to me that was part of her charm — she was a real person, not a mannequin, and she tried to have fun. During one Christmas season, she kept wearing a red-and-green V-neck cardigan with an elf and a train on one side and a Christmas tree on the other. The first time I saw her in it, she had accessorized with a set of dangly Santa earrings. I will admit now that I was surprised when I saw her dressed like that for a holiday press preview. It occurred to me that Mrs. Reagan especially would never have worn such a sweater, although Barbara Bush might have — but the whole look really was endearing. She wore the sweater again a few times that holiday season, including to the Residence staff party, where my husband and daughter had a photograph taken with her. I really like that photo!

I think Mrs. Clinton's lack of a perfectly cohesive style reflected her eclectic personality and the fact that she didn't try to become something she wasn't. That may be thanks to advice she got from former First Lady Jacqueline Kennedy Onassis, which she wrote about in her memoir, *Living History*. Just a few days after President Clinton's inauguration, Mrs. Clinton flew to New York to talk to Mrs. Onassis about bringing up a child in the White House, maintaining a semblance of privacy, and fashion. Mrs. Clinton "asked her if I should just turn myself over to a team of famous consultants as some in the media recommended." Mrs. Onassis was horrified at that idea. "You have to be you," she told Mrs. Clinton. "You'll end up wearing someone else's idea of who you are and how you should look." This relieved Mrs. Clinton, who explained that, "with Jackie's tacit permission, I determined to continue having fun while not taking any of it too seriously."

The fashion choice of Mrs. Clinton's I most appreciated was her predilection for pantsuits. This might not sound like a big deal these days, but not long ago, that would have been entirely unacceptable. While Mrs. Reagan was first lady, a member of the Residence staff once wore pants to work, and Muffie Brandon (Mrs. Reagan's social secretary) told the women of the staff that we were never to do such a thing. "Ladies," she said, "we must *never* wear pants in the White House. We represent America's women and we must always be dressed appropriately." Even back in the '80s, it seemed to me to be a little antiquated to insist on skirts and dresses, especially given all the bending and lifting I was doing as a florist, but of course we all did as we were asked.

With each first lady I worked for, I noticed that the women who work in the White House tended to mimic her style. It was an unconscious thing, but I think we all wanted her to feel like we were on her wavelength. So when I saw Mrs.

Clinton in pantsuits and saw that her East Wing staff (which was nicknamed "Hillaryland" because all but one of them were women) often wore pants as well, I asked Gary Walters, the chief usher of the Residence staff, if we could do it, too, and we began wearing pants a few times a week. This was an enormous change for us, and life became quite a bit more comfortable. I also saved a fortune on pantyhose.

When it came to choosing flowers, tablecloths, and table settings, as I mentioned earlier, Mrs. Clinton was decisive. But while she always knew right away what she wanted when she saw samples, her style varied greatly. Sometimes she selected casual mixed flowers; other times she wanted very contemporary arrangements, and then the next time she'd choose something ultra-traditional. Designing for her was fun because my staff and I got to play with so many different colors, styles, and designs, and she was open to almost anything.

Mrs. Clinton's first social secretary, Ann Stock, a sophisticated lady with great style whose opinion I trusted implicitly, told me that Mrs. Clinton preferred strong, bold colors, especially reds and oranges, unusual varieties, and tropical flowers, and an assortment of candle styles (tapers and pillars) on the same table. She also told me that Mrs. Clinton loved patterned tablecloths, and encouraged me to include them among the options with sample setups. So although my experience had taught me that plain, elegant tablecloths usually look better as a backdrop for flowers, china, and crystal, especially when set against the décor of the various White House rooms, I did present patterned tablecloths for her to choose from — and she chose them quite often. But my job was to please the first lady — not to do things exactly as I liked them, but as she liked them.

Luckily, I was pleasantly surprised to learn that if you put enough elegant china, glassware, and flowers on any tablecloth, it can still look good and turn a room into a beautiful setting for guests.

The most important consideration for Mrs. Clinton when it came to setting tables was that everyone could see each other and communicate easily. "We've been to some dinners at the White House where the flowers were so tall we couldn't see across the table. I don't ever want that," she said.

"Got it," I replied. "No tall centerpieces!" We both smiled and, of course, I never used tall centerpieces for her.

Mrs. Clinton decorated the second floor in a style that was much more contemporary and colorful than any of her predecessors had used. In the Center Hall, she hung a huge painting with splashes of color by the abstract expressionist Willem de Kooning, and she added colorful and interesting souvenirs (assorted sculptures, small urns and jars, brightly painted wooden boxes) that she and President Clinton collected from overseas trips. Although most of the furniture belonged to the White House and was quite classic in style, putting the sculptures and souvenirs on the tables gave it more of an eclectic feeling. Kaki Hockersmith, her interior designer, came to visit every so often from Little Rock. She and Mrs. Clinton worked with the White House curators to borrow more contemporary artwork from the National Gallery of Art, and on many days I would notice that an old masterpiece that had been hanging there for years was gone and a new contemporary painting was in its place. Mrs. Clinton had a large and colorful shell-shaped glass bowl put on display on the center table in the Center Hall on the second floor, and I soon learned it was one of Dale Chihuly's strikingly whimsical designs. She turned the First Lady's Garden (the East Garden, opposite the Rose Garden) into a sculpture garden and filled it with contemporary American sculptures on loan from various American museums and artists. The sculptures changed every few months, and on my way to work I often cut through the East Colonnade (a main entrance to the White House) rather than take the alley next to our shop, just to see if there was anything new. The guests and the thousands of visitors to the White House entered along the East Colonnade corridor, too, so they also had an opportunity to see the rich array of unique sculptures.

Mrs. Clinton kept the palette of soft yellows that had been in the main Residence hallway, but she redecorated the kitchen, changing it from a yellow and gold color scheme with dark wood cabinets to whites and blues with light cabinets, which brightened the room considerably. She placed a new white kitchen table in front of the window overlooking the North Grounds of the White House and Pennsylvania Avenue, so the Clintons could have breakfast there as a family and enjoy the view.

Mrs. Clinton also redecorated the second-floor dining room, changing the heavy hand-painted historical wallpaper to a more contemporary soft green silk moiré. (The wallpaper was never removed, which made the curators happy. It was just covered up with silk panels, which remained in place until Laura Bush changed it to a light gold damask fabric.) Her choice brightened the room and made it seem larger. And it was easier for me to coordinate centerpieces and tablecloths with the décor, because I no longer needed to consider the many colors in that original wallpaper.

## Gestures of Kindness

Mrs. Clinton shows a no-nonsense demeanor to the public, but behind the scenes she is thoughtful and generous. Throughout the time we worked together, she did more little things to make me feel appreciated than anyone else I'd ever worked for.

In the summer of 1993, I had to take a few days off from work for emergency surgery. I was gone for such a short time that I didn't think Mrs. Clinton would even realize I was absent. While I was recuperating, I was surprised to receive flowers and a note from her — not on official stationery, but on a card with a picture of a basket of flowers on the front. It said, "Nancy — A big bouquet for you from the president and me. We're wishing you a speedy and full recovery. I miss you — Hillary."

A few months later, a photographer took a picture of me for the *Washingtonian,* a local magazine. Shortly after the

A card Mrs. Clinton sent me when I was recuperating from emergency surgery.

magazine came out, the photo from the magazine, framed in gold, arrived for me in the flower shop. With it was a lovely note from Mrs. Clinton that said, "This is a photo from *House Beautiful* [it was actually the *Washingtonian*, but I didn't correct her!] I had framed for you. Hope you like it — I love the flowers and you! Hillary."

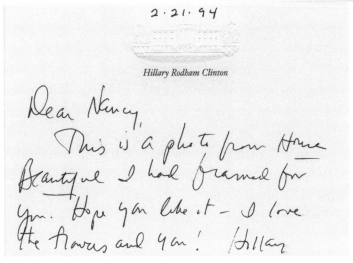

*Mrs. Clinton sent this note with a framed photo of me that had appeared in the* Washingtonian, *February 21, 1994.*

For Mrs. Clinton's first Christmas, the theme was angels, and hundreds of artists from around the country sent us almost 7,000 angel-inspired ornaments, made of fabric, glass, wood, metal, and other media in all different shapes and sizes. (After Christmas, many of the pieces we'd received from the artists were displayed at the National Museum of American Art for several months.) Working with artists was such a success — judging by the overwhelmingly positive feedback in the press and from White House visitors and guests — that Mrs. Clinton used outside American artists to design ornaments for the

Blue Room tree from then on. Once the holiday decorations were in place, the first lady always hosted a press preview. Before Mrs. Clinton's first holiday press preview in 1993, she and her press secretary and I stood together as we waited for more than one hundred members of the press to be ushered into the Blue Room. She was cool as a cucumber as always, but she didn't know quite what to expect. "You must have done this a hundred times," she said to me. "What will they ask?"

I explained that they would ask a few questions about the decorations and how and why she selected the angels theme. I said, "They might ask what you're getting the president and Chelsea, where the family is planning to spend Christmas, and then they might move on to current policy questions." The room was quiet for a moment while we waited. I noticed her earrings (green pavé bows with red pavé balls hanging from them) and thought they were charming, so I said, "Mrs. Clinton, you have on the cutest earrings." She smiled at me, and then the clamoring press began lining up in front of her, so that was the end of our conversation. The next morning, a little package arrived for me in the flower shop. Inside were the pavé bow earrings I'd complimented Mrs. Clinton on the day before. There was no note — but of course I knew exactly whom they were from.

That same Christmas, I had to work at the White House on Christmas Day itself. The flower shop staff rotated holiday duty, and it was my turn. Late in the morning, Mrs. Clinton called me in the flower shop to ask if I could come upstairs to the Yellow Oval Room for a minute. I could hear her laughing with the president as I walked down the hall, and when I arrived, they were both there, casually dressed and in festive moods. "Nancy, we have a present for you," she told me, and gave me a beautiful candle in a white ceramic container surrounded by three angels, a reference to the angel theme we'd used for the decorations. At Christmastime every year after that, she gave me a gift of a piece of jewelry — over the years I received a silver poinsettia brooch, a gold-eagle-on-pearl pin (which was like one she herself wore occasionally), a rhinestone-studded dragonfly pin, and a gold four-sided star with a black onyx center. I still have them all and wear them occasionally, especially the earrings during the holidays, and I love to tell my friends where I got them.

At Christmas a few years later, in the midst of an especially exhausting season of decorating and parties, I ran into Mrs. Clinton at the staff elevator in the pantry. She was waiting to go up and I was waiting to go down, and she looked about as worn out as I felt. She glanced over at me and then, out of the clear blue, she said, "I love you." I had been thinking about the next item on my to-do list and she caught me completely off-guard. I didn't know what to say. How do you respond when a first lady says, "I love you" to you? I blurted out, "I love you, too." She was definitely the only first lady to ever say that to me, and to me it felt like a genuine expression of her warmth and appreciation for all the hard work I'd been doing. We hugged as several butlers hustled past as they were getting ready for the next reception (they gazed at us without comment — but with raised eyebrows for sure). And then we both went on our way.

In January 1998, a news story broke that the president had had an affair with a twenty-two-year-old intern working in the West Wing. This was the first time I had learned anything about this particular situation, although of course all of us on the staff had heard about the president's alleged former indiscretions. A few weeks prior to the news story, the only rumor I had heard was that Mrs. Clinton had stopped an intern from going to the Oval Office so often. But I don't know who that intern was and never did find out.

Everyone on the staff was talking about the president's affair, and every day some new tidbit would appear in the news to keep the gossip flying: *Did you ever see her? When was she here? Do you know her? Where did she work?* Although I didn't have a great deal of interaction with Mrs. Clinton during the whole time when there was so much fallout from the affair, whenever I did see her in the Lower Cross Hall or on the second floor, she held her head high and acted as if nothing had happened. I admired her ability to keep her dignity, even though every night the press went on and on about the cigar story, the blue dress, whether the president had or hadn't had sex with Monica Lewinsky, and then, of course, the impeachment proceedings. The tempo in the White House changed and things became very low-key for a while. I imagined that deep down she must have been furious (I know I certainly would be if it were me), but she never showed those feelings to anyone on the staff. I heard insinuations from the press that she and the president had huge fights, but I never saw any of it and neither did my staff.

Incidentally, it was during the aftermath of the Lewinsky affair that Mrs. Clinton had what may have been her absolute best fashion moment. Anna Wintour, the editor-in-chief of *Vogue,* invited her to pose for the cover of the December issue. She wore a burgundy velvet dress by Oscar de la Renta, and in the photo (shot by Annie Leibovitz) I think she looked truly stunning. Mrs. Clinton later wrote in her memoir, "The experience did wonders for my spirits."

Plus, I got the chance to work with Annie Leibovitz, widely recognized as one of the world's best photographers! We designed the flowers for the photo shoot — Ms. Leibovitz wanted bright red roses, fully opened and casually arranged in one of the porcelain containers that we normally kept on the side tables in the Red Room.

Despite mood-lifters like the *Vogue* shoot, there were days when I could tell that Mrs. Clinton was distracted and kind of down, which was understandable. In addition to the normal stresses of being first lady, she had to cope with so many things at once: being a devoted mom to Chelsea and trying to protect her daughter's privacy, despite their fishbowl existence; soldiering on in the midst of the publicity that erupted over the Lewinsky affair; dealing with a host of accusations and allegations from those with their own agendas; and surviving the failure of her efforts to pass an unprecedented health care reform initiative. When she was upset, I could tell just by looking at her face and body language: she walked very stiffly, her shoulders were down, and she wasn't smiling. If that was the case, I usually feared that our interaction would go badly. But it never really did. Only once do I remember that her mood had a real bearing on one of our planning meetings. "Hi, Mrs. Clinton," I said. "How are you?" Her reply was a curt, "Not good." I never did find out what "not good" meant and I certainly wasn't going to ask. She simply selected the sample she liked and abruptly ended the meeting.

## But They Still Had Fun . . .

More than any other first family I worked with, the Clintons liked to party. A week rarely went by when we didn't have at least a small dinner or reception. There were several stretches of weeks (and occasionally, a month or more) when I worked on an event *every day*, including weekends, and didn't have a single day off. Some dinners included only five or six guests; other events were for several hundred people or more. During the fall and winter, we had a constant string of events, from small dinners and luncheons to receptions and large dinners and, of course, all the Christmas dinners, parties, and receptions. We were so overwhelmed with work during the second administration that I felt like I was totally neglecting my family. I even hired a personal chef for a few months to make us four or five dinners per week because I had no time to cook.

And then, during the spring and summer months, the Clintons got even busier! A tent went up on the South Lawn and stayed there for weeks on end, because the large parties kept happening every couple of days. (The first time we left the tent up for more than just a few days, we didn't realize it would kill the grass in so short an amount of time. It soon began to smell like a barn, so the next time we put up the tent, we removed the grass and replaced it when the tent came down.) There would be a congressional picnic, then a press picnic, then a dinner for Special Olympics, then an *In Performance at the White House*, a PBS event where guests came for dinner and enjoyed different types of musicals or performances by stars such as Elton John and Aretha Franklin. Elton John also performed together with Stevie Wonder at a 1998 dinner for British Prime Minister Tony Blair. This might sound glamorous to outsiders, but to us it meant endless and exhausting rounds of planning, setups, and cleanups.

Occasionally, I would meet the performers — I met Yo-

The lighter side of setting up for Christmas 1990: The president watches as Mrs. Bush tries on one of the giant toy soldier's hats for size.

Mrs. Bush and I share a laugh when we're supposed to be posing, but President Bush doesn't seem to mind. The exasperated photographer tried to get us to pay attention by saying, "Ladies . . ."

I'm setting the toy soldier's hat in place in the Old Family Dining Room in December 1990. I painted his cheerful face, which is a Styrofoam ball covered with plaster.

Mrs. Barbara Bush needlepointed this Raggedy Andy and Raggedy Ann from a pattern that I designed. They were a well-received addition to the Christmas tree in the Blue Room in December 1990.

In December 1990, we hung cookies all over the Christmas tree in the Oval Office. When President George H. W. Bush received visitors there, he'd give them cookies right off the tree. We were constantly replacing them so the tree wouldn't look bare.

President Bush stands in the Yellow Oval Room of the private residence, beside the family's personal Christmas tree, greeting a moose dressed for the holidays.

An electric train passes through a village made of needlepoint buildings at the base of the Christmas tree in the Blue Room in December 1991.

Mrs. Bush admires Santa's sleigh, which is actually a baby car seat that my staff adapted and reupholstered for Christmas 1991.

This is the view from the Grand Foyer into the Cross Hall, with the Blue Room Christmas tree visible in the doorway, in December 1991. Each decorated room had to have its own distinct character and look.

For the Camp David wedding of President George H. W. Bush and First Lady Barbara Bush's daughter, Dorothy (Doro), we decorated the patio outside the Aspen cabin for the reception dinner. The centerpieces were made of blush peonies, peach gerbera, and peach roses.

Chief Usher Gary Walters dumped a full box of shredded Styrofoam snow on my head! Volunteer Susan Madia (at back) and one of President and Mrs. Bush's grandchildren (foreground) had fun watching in December 1992.

Mrs. Bush takes time to thank more than 60 Christmas volunteers for pitching in, while her dog, Millie, sleeps in the middle of the floor, in December 1992.

During the Clinton administration, many parties were held outdoors in tents on the South Lawn. Their first major tent party was for the 25th reunion of Georgetown University's class of 1968, in June 1993.

Our theme for Christmas 1993 was angels, and this glorious tree was hung with unique angel ornaments made by artists all across the United States. The top of the tree was secured with a hook from the ceiling that usually held the chandelier.

My part-time staff members Dennis Rzaca and Ruth Loiseau
prepare apple and hydrangea centerpieces.

For an October 1994 state dinner to honor South African President Nelson
Mandela, we created an arrangement of pastel roses in vermeil containers and
decorated the head table with swags and jabots, which were one of Mrs. Clinton's
favorite design elements.

For Mrs. Clinton's birthday in October 1994, the theme was the 1950s — so I couldn't resist using hula hoops to frame white flower poodles in the center of the serving tables.

President and Mrs. Clinton pose with my daughter, Suzanne, my husband, Michael, and me in the Diplomatic Reception Room in December 1994. Just like the Second Floor Dining Room, this room features a breathtaking wallpaper mural.

Martha Stewart holds Socks, the Clinton's cat, as I show her around the East Room during the installation of Christmas decorations in 1995.

I was pleased to teach Chelsea Clinton and her friends the basics of putting together a flower arrangement. They were all fast learners.

President Clinton added a personal birthday greeting to the bottom of this photo of the first family with my husband, Michael, and me in December 1996. The odd thing is that my birthday isn't until May!

As my holiday volunteers gathered around in December 1997, Mrs. Clinton surprised me with an award for 20 years of service to the White House at Christmas. I had a hard time holding back the tears.

A holiday dinner in the Red Room in December 1997: crystal candelabra are filled with red roses and gold grapes, and the gold metallic tablecloths are set with the Johnson china.

Red or gold? I review the choices to help Mrs. Clinton decide on a tablecloth color for a Christmas dinner in December 1997. Behind me to the far right are Chief Usher Gary Walters and my assistant Wendy Elsasser. Mrs. Clinton's assistants are behind me to my left and right.

Mrs. Clinton (center) and I stand under the huge wreath, which decorates the outside of the White House and was the work of Robert Isabell (right), a wonderful New York designer. Our staff and holiday volunteers fill both stairways.

President Clinton studies the intricate Ice Palace that guest pastry chef Colette Peters fashioned out of a gum paste type of fondant icing in December 1998.

Here is a luminous holiday dinner in December 1998, with gold pillar candles on burgundy velvet tablecloths, red roses, gold glitter balls made by volunteers, and gold-banded china.

For the historic NATO 50th Anniversary Dinner in April 1999, a curved table was built for the East Room to seat 50 heads of state, and we had a tablecloth custom-made to match the carpet. The table is decorated with white hydrangeas, green grapes, white gardenias, white dendrobium orchids, and smilax foliage in vermeil containers with vermeil candlesticks.

For Mrs. Clinton I would create pen-and-ink drawings of each room and then, using a felt-tip pen, sketch in where the Christmas decorations would be installed.

My assistant Bob Scanlan stands in front of the remarkable Crystal Tree of Light, which was designed by Dale Chihuly for the Millennium Dinner on December 31, 1999.

For Christmas 2000, we decorated the foyer of the Cross Hall with holiday trees designed by Robert Isabell. When he passed away unexpectedly at 57, I lost a close friend.

Mrs. Clinton gives me one of her exuberant embraces after viewing the decorations for Christmas 2000. I treasure our special friendship to this day.

Yo Ma, Elton John, Stevie Wonder, Reba McEntire, Linda Ronstadt, Aaron Neville, Gladys Knight, Chet Atkins, Alison Krauss, and the Righteous Brothers while they were rehearsing during the afternoons before their respective events. (By the time the actual entertainment started in the evening, I was usually gone for the day.) I especially remember watching Elton John rehearse. He played his piano and sang on a stage in a tent while we were setting up. We stopped to listen, and I was struck by his incredible playing and stunning voice. He's unbelievably talented. Another time, when Jon Bon Jovi was rehearsing in a tent, one of my part-time designers went to the front of the stage with her camera. I saw her and immediately ran across the tent to tell her, "We don't allow guests to be photographed while they are in the White House." She had been unaware of the rule; I had been remiss in not giving her a heads-up before the event. She put her camera back in her pocket and apologized many times over, but I think she got a good picture of him anyway.

Often, when we had a tent party planned, I'd see clouds building up above the Oval Office just around 4:00 p.m. Summer afternoon rainstorms are very typical in Washington, and when I saw the clouds I knew the deluge was coming, but the parties happened anyway. My staff and I often sloshed through wet grass to set up dinner centerpieces or get cabaret tables ready for a party. Once we had so much rain, the pieces of the wooden floor in the tent started to wash away as water overflowed the gutters from all sides. The guests didn't seem to mind and later I overheard them saying how much fun it had been, wet shoes and all.

Aside from the very large dinners in tents, Mrs. Clinton

also liked smaller dinners and held them in many different rooms throughout the White House. Once, we had a long formal table with two vermeil candelabra and three vermeil containers filled with cream roses and blue delphinium over an antique lace tablecloth (so old I had to sew it together in places where it was coming apart) in the Blue Room for President Jacques Chirac of France and twenty guests. Sometimes Mrs. Clinton wanted to use the Red Room, the Green Room, or the lovely second floor Yellow Oval Room, one of four oval rooms in the White House complex, which many of the previous first ladies had also liked to use. We liked that she changed the locations of her dinners, because it gave us a chance to design in different color palettes.

Mrs. Clinton also liked to host parties that were more casual and festive than those previous first ladies had hosted, and when she did, she wanted us to have fun with decorations. For a Halloween party, we made ghosts from cheesecloth dipped in fabric stiffener. For her birthday celebrations, we planned theme parties, and the guests — and the first lady and president — came in costume. One year the guests and the staff dressed up as historical figures. Mrs. Clinton wore a black wig and a hoopskirt and dressed up as Dolley Madison, whom she called "one of my first lady heroines." Another year we threw a '50s party where everyone wore cat-eye glasses and saddle shoes, and we decorated the serving tables with standing hula hoops that had white flower poodles in the center. At yet another costume party, Mrs. Clinton donned a cowboy hat and a curly blonde wig to impersonate Dolly Parton.

The largest event I worked on during my thirty years in the White House was the NATO 50th Anniversary Summit in

April 1999. For this weeklong summit we had to decorate for events at the White House, as well as at the Reagan Center, the Mellon Auditorium, and Blair House (the presidential guesthouse across the street from the White House). We had to prepare for dinners, luncheons, meetings, a special dinner for fifty heads of state (and only the heads of state — no spouses), and an enormous dinner for 800 guests on the South Lawn the final day of the summit. I worked with Capricia Marshall on all the different events. Capricia is a beautiful lawyer, very efficient and on top of things. She was the social secretary during the second Clinton administration and is now Chief of Protocol for the Obama administration. We also worked with Robert Isabell, a designer from New York, who had a wonderful talent for creating spectacular events, especially in tents. He helped us plan the huge South Lawn dinner.

For the heads of state dinner, at which the world leaders were to be seated together, the Residence staff carpenters custom built a single, large curved table for fifty that perfectly fit in the East Room, the only room in the White House big enough to hold such a piece. We had a custom tablecloth made in pale green damask to fit the table, and we set it with the Truman china. The flower arrangements were a mix of white roses, white hydrangea, gardenias, green grapes, and white orchids. It was one of the most beautiful dinners I ever created in thirty years. (Mrs. Clinton was very involved in all of the NATO events — she looked at samples for every event. I remember she told me, "We have so much going on, and I really want everything to be beautiful.") For the 800-guest closing party, Robert designed the interior of the tent (which we were told to call a palladium, so it didn't sound so much like, well, a tent) with mirrored panels, crown moldings, and lights beaming from the floor to the ceiling, and a single head table to seat all fifty heads of state. It certainly didn't feel like being in a tent. It was stunning.

When all the NATO events were over, and everything was cleaned up, and the heads of state were returning home, I happened to be working on the third floor when Mrs. Clinton came out of one of the rooms. She looked at me and started clapping. Working with her for eight years, I learned that she always claps when she is happy. She exclaimed, "We did it! We did it! We did it!" We spoke for a few minutes about how well everything had gone at every one of the events, and how relieved we were that we'd gotten through it. "I think we made it through everything without even a minor disaster," I said. With a big smile, she replied, "We sure did."

To bring in the year 2000, we had a huge New Year's Eve party to celebrate the new millennium. Down came the Christmas decorations, and up went everything for the New Year. The tent came down on the South Lawn, but two more went up — one over the Rose Garden and one over the East Garden. Thankfully for all of us who were designing centerpieces, the weather was warm enough that we could work outside in the alley next to our shop. Phalaenopsis orchid plants (tall, thin stems with multiple white orchids with soft yellow centers, arching blooms) streamed in from every wholesaler in the area, and we repotted them in silver-painted ceramic bowls, then added white roses and adorned each pot with shiny silver glass balls. We placed these on iridescent white velvet tablecloths.

The guests at this party were invited for dinner, then to go to the Mall for the fireworks, and then to return to the

White House for a late supper and entertainment. Once everyone had temporarily left to see the fireworks (around 11:00 p.m.), we added more cabaret tables to both tents in time for the late-night party. To help with all the extra work, my daughter, Suzanne (who was home from college), and my dearest friend, Sharon Lewis, were working with me. As midnight approached, the tables were ready with flowers in place, the kitchen had everything in portable ovens ready to go, and the cleanup was finished. Before all the guests returned, Gary Walters invited the Residence staff to the roof to watch the fireworks. He brought several cases of champagne, and as the fireworks shot over our heads, my daughter, my friend, and I raised our glasses as the bells started to chime to ring in the New Year. It was certainly a memorable way to celebrate the start of a new millennium.

One weekend toward the end of the Clinton administration, I volunteered for weekend duty so the person who usually worked weekends for the flower shop could attend an event. At 9:00 a.m., I went to the second floor as we usually did during the week. I stepped off the staff elevator and peeked out (which I always did in case the first lady was with a guest in the West Hall or on the phone, so as not to interrupt her). The door leading to Mrs. Clinton's bathroom was directly across the West Hall from where I was, and I saw her run totally naked from her bathroom to the bedroom. We looked at each other and we both screamed. She ran into her bedroom and I immediately jumped back on the elevator and headed downstairs to my shop. I was so embarrassed and didn't really know what to say when I saw her next. When I ran into her later that afternoon (she was fully clothed this time!), we both laughed about it. She said it was like living in her sorority house again.

## After the Storm

When Mrs. Clinton decided to run for senator of New York, she was gone from the White House quite a bit, especially the closer the election got. If she came back to the White House and I showed her a sample, she made her decisions more quickly than ever, and moved on to the next agenda item for the day. When she was gone, Capricia, who had a great eye and knew Mrs. Clinton's style well, could sign off on things.

The very end of the Clinton administration was relatively turmoil-free after the impeachment hearing was finally over. Whenever I happened to see President and Mrs. Clinton together on the second floor or in the Lower Cross Hall, they appeared to be happy and relaxed, even acting kind of silly or affectionate with each other. I never really saw any arguments or tension between them. Although many articles appeared in the press that described them throwing things or having screaming matches, as I mentioned earlier, I never ever saw anything like that. What's more, I never heard about such things either, not even through internal White House gossip.

I didn't have much direct contact with President Clinton because he was in the Oval Office during the week and we were always careful not to bother the first family on the weekends. If we did have to be there on the weekends, we tried to go to the second floor only during those times when he went jogging or ran over to the Oval Office for a few minutes. We tried to do this with all the presidents, to give them privacy. (When you have a day off and you're relaxing at home, would you want someone you didn't really know hanging around watering your flowers?) So we always checked with the ushers' office, who knew where the president was at all times. But when I did see President Clinton, he was always friendly and said hello. The day before he left office, I was standing outside the ushers' office door, where the elevator from the Residence opens up on the state floor. He saw me and said, "Nancy, I was just looking for you. I wanted to give you this," and handed me a gold Cross pen-and-pencil set in a black case. (I don't think he was actually looking for me — he just happened to run into me and gave me what he was carrying, which was a nice gesture.) I said, "Thank you so much, Mr. President." And that was it. Although I don't ever use it — I think of it as more of a keepsake — it's still in my desk drawer.

After Mrs. Clinton left the White House, she returned for meetings in the West Wing during the Bush administration. During her first visit, someone from the ushers' office called to tell me she had asked, "Where's my rock star flower shop?" and of course my staff and I all came running to say hello. We hugged each other and she asked how I was doing. "Great," I said. "How are *you* doing?" She laughed and replied, "Very busy!" Though I have not kept in touch with Mrs. Clinton, as I have with other former first ladies, I am so proud of all she's achieved. Her career path — senator, leading presidential candidate, now secretary of state — is something we're unlikely to see from many first ladies.

# Quiet Elegance: Laura Bush

*When home is a grand museum filled with an entire nation's history, it could be a bit cold and intimidating — all that marble! But because of Nancy Clarke and her wonderful staff at the White House, we were greeted every day with the warmth and beauty of incredible flowers. Nancy's artistry and understanding of White House events gave her a sure touch with every assignment, from state dinners to children's parties to the Fourth of July. The arrangements brought delighted comments from thousands of visitors.*

*The magic of the White House florists was at its best during the Christmas season. Under Nancy's leadership and with the help of volunteers from around the U.S., this crew transformed every part of the building into a treat for eye and spirit. I was always amazed by the creations of papier-mâché the florists made to go with each year's theme. Of course, our favorites were the papier-mâché Barney and Miss Beazley! I cherish many memories of working with Nancy and I'm grateful to count her as a friend.*

*— Laura Bush*

I first met Laura Bush — and her daughters — on January 20, 1989, George H.W. Bush's Inauguration Day. The entire Bush family was in Washington for the inaugural balls, and my staff and I stayed late at the White House to pitch in with breaking down moving boxes, taking out garbage, and everything else that had to be finished. While I was doing that, Chief Usher Gary Walters asked me if I could watch the Bushes' twin daughters, Jenna and Barbara, who were seven years old at the time and had grown tired of sitting and watching the parade go by. Of course I said I would.

Jenna was more outgoing, friendlier, and more talkative at first. Barbara was much quieter, but she warmed up and both of them started asking me questions: "Do you always work at the White House? Do you have any children? How old are they?" That kept them entertained for a few minutes, but we needed an *activity*. The flower shop didn't exactly have toys they could play with, so I took them up to their guest bedrooms. Once we were there, I told them to look carefully at the colors of the walls, rugs, and furnishings, because they were going to make their very own flower arrangements as decorations for their rooms.

Back in the flower shop, they each selected a small vase and then started choosing flowers. For the next hour or so, they worked intently, running back and forth getting more flowers and exchanging colors. When they were both finally finished, we went to their bedrooms to see how their arrangements made their rooms look. Jenna thought her arrangement looked perfect in her room, and pointed out how well the colors she had chosen matched the colors in the room; Barbara still didn't say much, but she smiled when I complimented her on her beautiful choice of flowers.

"Thank you," Laura Bush said to me the next day. "That was the most wonderful way to welcome the girls to the White House." Of course, I didn't know at the time that they would be calling the White House home twelve years later.

When the girls were at the White House on subsequent visits to "Gampy," as they called their grandfather, they came into the flower shop five or six times a day to play with the flowers. They were taking them to Barbara Bush (we found wilted flowers in water glasses all over the second floor Residence after they visited). I saw Laura Bush occasionally during those visits as well, but only very briefly. She would say hello and not much else, if she happened to be on the second floor while I was there. Though she was always very well dressed and polite, she was not really talkative, so I didn't feel I knew her at all when George W. Bush was elected in 2000.

The 2000 election was quite unusual, with the question of the hanging chads, the Florida recount, and eventually the Supreme Court's decision. For the Residence staff, the delay in election results meant we had no idea who would be coming into office, so I searched for whatever I could find online, in newspapers and magazines, or on television, to get a feeling of what either potential first lady (Mrs. Bush or Mrs. Gore) would be like. How did they dress? What were their favorite colors? What causes did they support? Anything at all to get a better read on the style and sensibility of whoever would be first lady, so I could be prepared with ideas for samples and arrangements for events early in the new president's administration. The chefs did the same thing, trying to learn their favorite foods, eating habits, and what kinds of restaurants they frequented. The housekeepers wanted to know how neat the first lady would be, and whether she liked a little family clutter or was stringent about having everything in its place. This was all we talked about for weeks. We had met Laura Bush when she had visited, but we had no idea what it would be like to work for her. We knew Mrs. Gore a bit from her time in Washington during the Clinton years, and we heard rumors about the Gores being big party people, so I started mentally preparing for that. We'd just had eight years of planning huge event after huge event, and I was tired! But we just did not know, not for weeks. When the decision was finally made, I think everyone was relieved. Most of us had at least met the Bushes, and they also knew how things worked in the White House, so we weren't quite starting from scratch the way we typically did at the beginning of a new administration.

On George W. Bush's Inauguration Day in January 2001, most of the extended Bush family was at the White House again. Former First Lady Barbara Bush happened to be getting off the elevator just as I was coming around the corner. We hugged, and she said, "Thank goodness you're still here!" I said, "Oh, Mrs. Bush, I'll always be here." She replied, "Well, you will be for the next eight years. You're going to love Laura." It took me a while to understand what she meant, because Laura Bush was so reserved and even standoffish at first, with a more subdued personality than any other first lady I've worked for. But over time, as we got to know each other better, we developed a strong, if quiet, bond, especially during our planning for Christmases and her daughter Jenna's wedding. And after she'd been in the White House for several years, we reached the point where we knew what the other was thinking before either of us said a word.

## Getting Started

My first interaction with Mrs. Bush as first lady was the second day after she moved in. I saw her on the second floor and asked her if there was anything in particular that she would like us to do in terms of floral arrangements for the Residence. "For the time being," she said in her soft Texas drawl, "why don't you keep doing the same flowers that you did for Mrs. Clinton, and I'll let you know if I want you to change anything."

Some first ladies didn't care when we came to the second floor to do our work, but Mrs. Bush requested that we arrive promptly at 8:00 in the morning, which would be before any of her meetings, coffees, or teas in the Residence began. The president was an early riser; his butlers always came in very early, because he got up around 5:00 a.m. to let his dogs out on the South Grounds, and he was long gone to work by 8:00 a.m. By then, Mrs. Bush had eaten breakfast (usually a bowl of cereal) and was dressed for the day. Everyone from the different staffs — maids (who take care of making the beds, dusting, and laundry), housekeepers (who do vacuuming and deeper cleaning), engineers, plumbers, Dale Haney from the National Park Service (who cared for all the plants), and at least one of us from the flower shop — arrived at the same time. We usually crossed paths as we worked quickly to change the flowers, water the plants, and vacuum, and everyone was finished in about an hour or so. While we were there, Mrs. Bush was often in one of the chairs in the West Sitting Hall near the phone, drinking her coffee, usually by herself and occasionally with a member of her staff. Sometimes she flipped through her schedule or went over her next speech, or she was often on the phone with her East Wing staff. "Good morning" or "I love the flowers on the coffee table" might have been the only comment she made to me, and sometimes I didn't see her at all.

In February 2001, I worked on my first very small dinner for Mrs. Bush — I arranged flowers for a dinner for four at Camp David, when British Prime Minister Tony Blair came for a working visit. I created a sample of mixed varieties and an assortment of colors for her, as I typically would have made for Mrs. Clinton at Camp David, and she signed off on it. But I later found out it wasn't her style at all. When her interior decorator, Ken Blasingame, came to visit in early March 2001, to help her redecorate the second and third floors of the White House, he told me about the arrangements Mrs. Bush liked best — big, full, yet simple arrangements that featured just a single type of flower, or were monochromatic. I thought back to the first sample and realized it was totally wrong because I used so many different types of flowers, and a mix of reds and golds to match the color scheme Mrs. Clinton had at Camp David. There were too many colors and too many kinds of flowers, and it wasn't clean and simple enough for Mrs. Bush. It always bothered me a little that she didn't mention it at the time. I think she signed off on the first arrangement because she is very polite — and at the beginning of the administration she was probably a little uncomfortable dealing with her new staff. As she became more comfortable with us, if we placed an arrangement or showed her samples she didn't care for, she was still polite about it, and would simply say, "That's not my style" or "That's not my taste" and then tell us what she preferred instead. "Make it bigger" and "use more flowers" were the directions she gave most often. We joked in the flower shop that we were now doing Texas-sized flower arrangements, which we enjoyed doing because we knew it was what she wanted.

I quickly learned that Laura Bush is meticulous in everything she does, and when it came to matters of aesthetics (home décor, clothes, personal appearance), she wanted everything to be *perfect,* which in some ways was similar to Mrs. Reagan's style. However, Mrs. Bush had more hands-on involvement in making sure things were just so. Whenever she had guests staying at the White House, she personally did a walk-through to double-check the guest rooms, and often I accompanied her so I could make sure the flowers we put together would coordinate with the rooms to her liking. When we entered a bedroom, she would point to a chair or the draperies and ask me to match the flowers to them. After we did the flowers, she would check the rooms again. Sometimes, everything was fine; other times, she would move arrangements from room to room or ask us to redo them altogether if the color combination wasn't quite right or an arrangement needed more greenery. I often saw her adjust the books on the nightstand or move the guest soap dish over so it looked more centered.

After Mrs. Bush redecorated the Library on the ground floor, adding vibrant striped draperies and a brighter rug, she told me exactly what kind of flowers she wanted us to keep in there, and then she and her interior designer came into the Library to watch me put together the first arrangement for the room, pointing out precisely which shade of rose should go where. My staff ran back and forth, bringing the different shades they requested. Once we had created an arrangement that met her specifications, we used a carbon copy of it every single week. Mrs. Bush liked us to keep the arrangements the same from week to week in every room she redecorated (the Library, the Vermeil Room, and the Green Room), as long as the flowers were in season.

When I showed her sample flower arrangements and table settings to select for a dinner, she often moved blossoms an inch or two within the arrangements or smoothed out the tablecloth so it looked better. Occasionally, she would mention to me that the carpet in the Dining Room needed to be cleaned again, which I always passed on to housekeeping because I had nothing to do with cleaning the carpets. So I would just agree with her (because she was usually right). She kept the furniture in the Residence aligned just so, and I frequently saw her adjusting chairs to make sure their legs were appropriately lined up with the boards of a wood floor, making sure all the paintings were perfectly straight on the walls, or moving lampshades to ensure they were even. The second and third floors of the White House were always beautiful and spotless.

As a florist, whenever I tended to the flowers, I ran the risk of water dribbling from the watering can, or of causing containers to overflow and spill onto antique tables, or of dropping little pieces of leaves or petals. Because Mrs. Bush was so fastidious, when I was working for her I always worried we may have left a mess somewhere that she might find. Luckily, she never did because when that happened and I missed it, the butlers (or Maria, her personal housekeeper from Texas, who moved to the White House with the Bushes) would clean it up for me — and then I would hear about it later from whomever had cleaned it up.

## A Woman of Simple and Elegant Style

Mrs. Bush went to the White House beauty shop almost every morning to have her hair and makeup done. This was something she paid for herself. "I really felt for Hillary Clinton," she explained in her memoir, "who spent years having the press write nasty things about her hairstyles. It unnerved me enough that I paid with our own money for someone to come to the White House and blow-dry my hair . . . just so I could avoid having a bad hair day."

She was always simply and elegantly dressed, usually in silk slacks and plain, beautiful sweaters for everyday and silk suits for events. As she wrote in her memoir, "I'm not one who follows each season's new trends; I have been wearing the same suits, sweaters, and slacks for years." For state dinners and other formal occasions, she wore simple, beautiful gowns or long skirts with a beaded blouse or jacket. Her look was always classic, but that doesn't mean it was boring. The afternoon before her first state dinner, for Mexico, she brought the dress she planned to wear into the dining room from the beauty shop so she could show it to me. It was an elegant yet bold Arnold Scaasi dress of red lace over hot pink silk. President Bush happened to walk into the dining room while we were looking at it.

"Bushie, what are you doing?" he asked. (He often called her Bushie.)

"We're looking at my dress for the dinner," she replied.

"*That's* what you're wearing?" he said, as if a bit taken aback. "What about black?"

"It's Mexico — I'm going to wear something bright," she said, smiling.

"Well," he said teasingly, "I think you should wear a black one."

Mrs. Bush and I rolled our eyes at each other but didn't say anything. Of course she wore the hot pink dress — and looked gorgeous in it.

I never saw her wear jeans, except in photos taken at the family's ranch in Texas. She almost always wore jewelry — often simple, short necklaces, sometimes with silver or gold accents, a single string of pearls, or multiple strands of single-colored stones. My favorite necklace of hers was a short strand of large turquoise stones. Her earrings were usually small pearl studs or small earrings that matched her necklace.

Having the Bushes in the White House was a striking contrast to having the Clintons there. The Clintons were extravagant entertainers with huge personalities, and they hosted events day after day and night after night. Things slowed down significantly when George W. Bush took office. As a couple, the Bushes were quieter, less likely to entertain on a large scale, and more likely to go to bed early (usually before 10:00 p.m.). Even on inauguration night, they were home before midnight. When they did entertain, they tended to have smaller dinner parties in the parlors (the Red Room, Green Room, or Blue Room). Sometimes they would show a movie in the theater and invite guests for a buffet dinner, and sometimes they just served popcorn and drinks. For the most part, aside from official functions, any entertaining they did was extremely low-key. And then, only nine months into the administration, the terrifying attacks of 9/11 took place and everything changed.

## 9/11

On the morning of September 11, 2001, my staff and I were getting ready for a congressional barbecue, putting together centerpieces in the alley next to our shop. Just as I returned to the flower shop, the phone rang; my retired assistant was calling to tell us to turn on the television immediately. The minute we did, we were horrified to see the first plane hit the World Trade Center tower (and they showed it over and over again) and the terrible flames engulfing the building, the smoke billowing up, and people running and screaming. Quickly, I ran up to the ushers' office and asked them to turn their TV on, too. Gary Walters, who was the White House chief usher, was standing next to me when we saw the second plane hit the second tower. He said it must be a terrorist attack and ran out of the office. I didn't know what to think at that point, so I ran back downstairs to my staff.

At the same time, the uniformed Secret Service officers were getting directions on their phones in the back hall next to our shop. They had already gotten the word to my staff to evacuate the White House. There was no time for anything, not even to get our personal belongings. "Just go!" they shouted. When they tried to send me out the doorway, I ran back into the flower shop anyway because I did not have my purse or car keys with me. It took a split second and I was back out into the hallway. This time, twenty or more Secret Service officers were running toward the door, too. They were coming from everywhere, from upstairs and downstairs, because this hall doorway was a major exit. Everyone was yelling, "Run!" They were all dressed in black and some had what looked like little machine guns at their sides. I did what I was told and ran with them. There was no time to think about what we were doing. We just did it. As I ran with the officers toward the exit gate at the fence line, another Secret Service agent was yelling, "Go north, go north!" to everyone coming out the gate because they'd just learned that a plane had crashed into the Pentagon, too. (While this was going on, my assistant, Wendy, was working on the second floor. Although she had no idea what was going on at the time, when she looked out the window she could see the smoke coming from the plane that had just hit the Pentagon.)

I think the last time the White House had been attacked was in 1814, when the British burned the White House, so the Residence staff had had no evacuation plan in place. It was chaos.

Out on the street, public transportation in the city was free, but traffic was completely gridlocked because all the buildings surrounding the White House were evacuated too. I started to walk and realized, as I went to open up my purse to look for some change so I could use a pay phone, that I was shaking inside. My hands were trembling and I didn't even know it. People were crowding the streets, walking in every direction. Some were crying, others were talking anxiously, distressed about the plane hitting the Pentagon. Some said the State Department was hit too (which was not true), but nobody really knew what just happened. I headed to Georgetown one mile away, where my husband worked, and by the time I got there, everything was closed down. Some shops had signs written on plain white paper and taped to their doors that just said "Closed"; others were completely dark. I found a gas station with a phone booth outside and called my husband. (I didn't have a cell phone yet! Not that cell phones were working that day anyway.) My husband picked me up and once we got away from the District, the roads were practically deserted, but I still could not settle down. My hands were still shaking. Even now, as I write this, it sickens me to think about what happened to our country that day.

When the attacks occurred, Mrs. Bush was attending a meeting on Capitol Hill. She is always escorted by the Secret Service, and they immediately took her to a safe house. Fortunately, everyone on the Residence staff was okay, but many of us had friends or neighbors who worked in the Pentagon who were hospitalized or killed that day. My husband often went to the Pentagon for work, so we received dozens of phone calls that day from people checking in to see if he was okay.

Mrs. Bush was back in the White House by the time I returned to work on September 12. She had the ushers' office ask us to rearrange the flowers that had been intended for centerpieces for the congressional picnic into hundreds of small arrangements to be delivered to people in the hospital who had been injured in the attack. Everyone returned to work the next day, because no one knew what else to do and no one had told us to stay home. Of course we were stunned, sad, and worried about friends we hadn't heard from at the Pentagon — and what might happen next. In the days following the attacks, when Mrs. Bush saw us, she asked what happened to each of us that day and how we were doing now. She personally thanked Keith, one of the designers on my staff, for helping Maria, her housekeeper, find a place to go since she lived at the White House and couldn't go back that day. He lived on Capitol Hill a few miles away, and had invited several members of the staff to go home with him.

The president, who had been in Florida, returned to the White House the evening of September 11, and the next day, unbelievably, the White House hosted public tours. Everyone was trying to act normal because we didn't know what else to do. But by September 13, everything was shut down. The president spent most of his days and nights in the West Wing, so I didn't see him, but I did see Mrs. Bush and noticed she was trying to act calm around the staff. But we were still very jumpy.

Not long after September 11, a plane strayed into

the White House airspace, which triggered a "shelter in place" alert from the Secret Service. The entire staff, still frightened and on edge about the recent tragedy, ran into the bunker beneath the White House — and so did the president. He remained completely composed and reassuring, and asked people standing close to him if they were okay and if everyone else they knew was okay. He inquired specifically about Maria, his housekeeper, and he wanted to know where his dogs were. Members of the staff assured him everyone was fine. Most of the ninety-six people on the Residence staff working at the White House that day made it into the bunker. I was standing about twenty feet away from the president and could hear him talking in a calm, reassuring voice to people near him. His Secret Service agents, who stayed near him at all times, were updating him on what was actually going on, and within two or three minutes, it was over. (It turned out to be nothing significant, just a pilot who accidentally flew off course.) This experience gave me a new appreciation of the president. On television he was always calm and in control, but to see him under these highly stressful circumstances and to realize he was calm and in control gave me great comfort.

For months following the attacks, only staff members and invited guests were allowed into the White House. And for all workers and visitors, security clamped down. To get into work every day, I had to go through two checkpoints and have my car searched (with a detection dog) just to get to my parking place. And then as everyone, guests or staff, entered the gate into the actual White House, we all had to run our purses and bags through a scanner. Those security protocols are still in place today.

At Christmastime, when we usually had endless parades

of public tours coming to see the elaborate decorations, the White House was opened to television cameras only. "That season," Mrs. Bush wrote in her memoir, "the White House had the quality of stillness after a snow."

## Big Events, Big Changes

The attacks of September 11 took place early in the Bush presidency. Tours almost vanished for an entire year, the calendar was cleared of many upcoming events, and our pace of work slowed dramatically. And I realized Mrs. Bush was still finding her niche as first lady. Having observed different administrations firsthand over time, I've noticed that in the first two or three years first ladies are usually noncontroversial and more conservative (in style, that is — politics are another story). This was certainly true of Mrs. Bush, and I think it was reflected in her taste in flowers. When I showed her sample flowers for events, she went right for soft pastel shades and traditional styles for both tablecloths and flowers. She got a little more adventurous when we had state dinners (which was not too often, because the president seemed to prefer meeting heads of state at the Texas ranch). The social secretary told me that Mrs. Bush liked to incorporate elements related to the country. So for a state dinner for Mexico, for instance, we worked real limes — an important Mexican product — into the centerpieces. For a state dinner to honor Polish President Kwasniewski and his wife, Mrs. Bush wanted the color scheme to be red and white, like Poland's flag. For the most part, though, she stuck to the basics until late in the first term.

By February 2004, I had the sense that Mrs. Bush was starting to feel more confident. She had begun to lean in a more contemporary direction after some successes with the occasional brighter shades or choice of unusual flowers. So when we made samples for the Governors' Dinner, I created an arrangement that was *very* bright — hot pink anemones with a fuchsia tablecloth — and waited to see what would happen. She selected a different sample initially, but then the next morning she called the flower shop from the second floor and asked me to bring up the colorful arrangement that I'd presented the day before. I put the tablecloth down with the flowers on top and showed her a base plate from the red Reagan china collection. I thought the vivid colors were an exciting change of pace. She looked at it from all angles, backed up to see it better from a distance, and finally asked, "Nancy, what do you think?" Forgetting for a moment to whom I was speaking, I replied, almost impatiently, "Oh, just do it!" And she did. The evening of the dinner, the Residence staff working in the dining room gasped when they saw the colors — shocking pink with the red china — but the dinner was a huge success. The butlers working the dinner passed on compliments they overheard the guests make about the flowers, and the social secretary, Cathy Fenton, told me about the many phone calls she received the next day from guests who wanted to say how beautiful the dinner was. After that, Mrs. Bush started selecting hotter colors much more often.

And then when President Bush won reelection in November 2004, I noticed even more of a change in Mrs. Bush. Just as her floral choices were brightening, her mood seemed brighter and happier as well. Her clothes were more colorful, too. I felt as though she was really starting to relax as first lady. She engaged in more small talk with my staff and me instead of simply answering our questions or giving us directions. She asked about my daughter's wedding and how the plans were coming, and one day she told Wendy, my assistant, that she had on "cute shoes," which became a joke in our shop. Whenever anyone (male or female) on my staff wore new shoes, everyone would say, "Cute shoes."

She also made some big decisions concerning the East Wing White House staff. Just before Christmas, she hired a new social secretary, Lea Berman, a well-known Washington hostess and event planner. Lea was very focused and efficient, and I found her intimidating at first. She rarely liked the arrangements we made, and she often took them off the tables (when we were already set up for a function) to be redone. She brought pictures and magazine photos of floral designs for me — she liked arrangements tightly packed with flowers, more formal than what we'd been doing — and took recipes she found in cookbooks to the kitchen, which none of the previous social secretaries had ever done. She stayed for less than two years — but she sure whipped the place into shape during her tenure. The kitchen started preparing the exact menus from Lea's suggested recipes; the operations staff (who move equipment into place for functions) learned exactly what she wanted in each room and how to place things to her precise specifications; and we redid arrangements over and over until we finally began to create arrangements that she would approve consistently.

Soon after Lea became social secretary, Mrs. Bush replaced Walter Scheib, who had been the White House executive chef since 1994. President Bush had never been a big fan of Walter's food, which was fancier than he liked. When Walter was fired, many of us on the staff worried that it was just the beginning of a big overhaul. I walked on eggshells for a while, as Lea didn't seem pleased with many of our color choices or the flower selections we used on a daily basis, and I thought maybe I might be on the list for overhaul, too. (There were no more firings after Walter, but it was still in the back of our minds for months.)

In July 2005, the White House hosted a state dinner with Prime Minister Manmohan Singh of India, which Mrs. Bush later told me was her favorite. (On the day before I retired, she called my cell phone to say congratulations and to thank me for my years of service. When she asked me what I'd be doing next, I told her I wanted to write a book about my White House experiences. "Be sure to include a photo of the elephant arrangements you did for the India dinner," she told me.) Lea Berman had found a picture of elephants made from flowers, and she asked if we could do a smaller version of that as a table centerpiece. So I bought elephant-shaped wire frames from a topiary company, which we filled with floral foam, and we used those as the foundation for making elephants from green button pom-pom chrysanthemums. Each elephant wore a saddle of hot pink floribunda roses with gold tassels and a draped headpiece of hypericum berries. When we showed Mrs. Bush the sample, she told me it was perfect and that we just had to do it, but only on every other table. She thought one on each table would be "too much." So we alternated the elephants with brightly colored circular flower arrangements. The effect was striking and so much fun.

For a state dinner honoring Emperor Akihito of Japan in June 2006, we again used the bold colors and contemporary lines Mrs. Bush was coming to love. By this time, when she walked into a room to view samples, I knew instantly (before she even spoke) which one she would select based on how she smiled and where her attention went right away. I also could tell when she was thinking, "That's not my taste," because she'd barely glance at samples that didn't interest her. In this case she walked straight over to a large ball of bright green cymbidium orchids atop tall clear glass cylinders on bright green dupioni silk cloths and said, decisively, "That one."

Amy Zantzinger, who had worked in the visitors office during George H.W. Bush's administration, took over for Lea Berman in February 2007. She was a little more easygoing than Lea had been, and she knew our style and skills well — and generally liked what we did. The first dinner she organized was for Queen Elizabeth. What a way for a new social secretary to get started! Amy spoke to Mrs. Bush frequently and relayed details to us about the guests who were invited, the kind of food Mrs. Bush wanted, and the style and colors of flowers she would like to see for samples. Amy was learning the ropes as a new social secretary, and all of us appreciated her input. It was a white-tie dinner, which is extremely formal, so the flowers had to be very formal, too. Amy also passed along the news that TV crews would be filming the dinner preparations behind the scenes. The tempo picked up in every shop. My staff and I had been filmed several times, so we weren't especially nervous, but we talked about when the crew was coming to our shop and what we needed to be working on and, of course, what we should wear (simple colors and no white, as it doesn't show well on camera).

When Amy and I showed Mrs. Bush samples, again I knew immediately which one she wanted. She headed right for the sample in which I used pieces from the

White House's classic vermeil collection — elaborate gold candelabra and wine coolers filled with pastel, cream, and white roses on an ivory damask cloth. That was exactly the one I thought she'd choose. By then, and for the rest of the Bush administration, we worked almost perfectly in sync.

## Christmases Bright and Beautiful

Every first lady gets involved with planning the White House Christmas decorations, but of all the first ladies I worked with, Mrs. Bush most loved being part of this process. She and I worked with her interior decorator, Ken Blasingame, who helped her redecorate much of the White House and design holiday displays. Ken and Mrs. Bush had been friends for years, decorating her house in Texas, having lunch together, going on shopping trips, and visiting friends. Ken was a big influence on her, and often the decisions she made regarding colors or styles were decisions they made together. Mrs. Bush and Ken always came up with a theme for the Christmas decorations, and then I had to figure out how we could translate what she wanted into doable decorations. Their ideas were often complicated, and this wasn't always easy. Thinking about how to execute some of their visions kept me awake many nights!

However, I found Ken to be delightful. He is tall, thin, and sophisticated, with an artistic air and a carefree manner, and he made me laugh. We could be having a serious meeting with Mrs. Bush and her East Wing staff and he would throw in an off-the-wall joke or make a funny drawing on my sketches that I had to show Mrs. Bush. When he arrived for a visit, he always came into our shop and gave me a kiss and a big hug. We seemed to be on the same wavelength about most things design-related, and we had lunch together if Mrs. Bush was busy, ordering takeout from the Navy Mess. (The fact that Mrs. Bush was such close friends with someone as fun and funny as Ken told me a lot about her — behind her proper, former-librarian facade is a warm, friendly woman who loves to joke and laugh. But only a few people ever really get to see that side of her.)

We usually started planning for Christmas almost a year in advance. I loved how excited Mrs. Bush got about Christmas. Until we worked together on her daughter's wedding in 2008, I felt my strongest connection to her was during our Christmas planning sessions, because it was so clear she loved what she was doing (and I definitely enjoyed Christmas all year long!).

Sometimes Mrs. Bush made me a little crazy with her detailed and specific requests (put this exact ornament here, that one there; make the bows a tiny bit bigger; reverse the colors of the ribbons). We had to plan and execute every tiny detail, from the color of lights in every room to which flowers to use to match the furniture. Mrs. Bush, Ken, and I always spent one entire day in the fall going through everything and walking from room to room with a bag of samples as possibilities. After she made a choice, she would glance over to Ken to get a nod of approval, and when he gave his blessing I quickly wrote everything down so we could move on to the next room.

In addition to planning the public Christmas decorations, Mrs. Bush decorated the first family's living quarters on the second floor of the White House with family-style decorations that she had used for years. She liked colored lights and had a collection of Christopher Radko's colorful, whimsical glass ornaments that she added to each year.

(There were many Santa Clauses in different designs, glass stockings, children, pets, and even a pumpkin.) Mrs. Bush loved her own velvet tree skirt, but it didn't quite make it around the bottom of the big tree, so we filled in the empty space with plain velvet fabric from our shop. She personally placed her collection of carved wooden and ceramic Santa Clauses on tables around the Residence, and on the big table near the entrance to the second floor, she placed her own crèche, with beautifully carved wooden figures.

Before 9/11 happened, Mrs. Bush had selected an all-white theme for the public decorations for Christmas 2001, including snowy trees in the Cross Hall and replicas of historical white houses from all over the United States. We were well under way in the creation of the decorations when 9/11 occurred, but Mrs. Bush thought this design would still work. She focused more on the creation of replicas of historical houses from the fifty states and presidential homesites, and called it "Home for the Holidays," celebrating the warmth and safety of home. Since the White House was closed to the public, Mrs. Bush allowed the press to come in and film television specials so the public could see the decorations.

Each year Mrs. Bush called on many different artists from around the country to design ornaments for the main Blue Room tree, to showcase their diverse talents. Twice we contacted the governors' offices in every state to ask them to select artists; one year we worked with 390 artists who created ornaments for each of the country's 390 national parks, and another year we had ornaments designed by artists from all of the country's different congressional districts. Each ornament was carefully designed and totally unique to the White House.

After the enthusiastic response to our presidential homesite replicas that were part of our 2001 decorations, in 2002, Mrs. Bush wanted to celebrate the pets the previous presidents had while they were living in the White House. We used papier-mâché to construct animals for the vignettes on the pier tables (elegant tables that sit against the walls in some of the public rooms of the White House). Mrs. Bush knew about many of the former pets and helped me with the research. Some pets were a little wacky: President Wilson had a ram named Old Ike (who reportedly chewed tobacco), John Quincy Adams had an alligator that Lafayette had given him, and Calvin Coolidge briefly kept a pet raccoon. Mrs. Bush asked me, "Where do you suppose they kept a raccoon?" and we both started to laugh. What was no laughing matter (at the time!) was the unexpected challenge posed by President Washington's horse, Nelson. I had the assignment of creating Nelson out of papier-mâché. Night after night, I worked on it in my kitchen, staying up until the wee hours until it was finally done. Exhausted, I stepped back to admire my handiwork . . . and then it promptly fell off my table. The tail slid off and sat in a pile of mâché on the floor, and half of Nelson's stomach just dropped away. I burst into tears out of sheer frustration. Then, after taking a deep breath, I got back to work and reassembled the horse sometime before dawn. When I brought Nelson in, he was a big hit. Overall, everyone loved the "Presidential Pets" theme as it gave such a unique glimpse into White House history, but oh, what a lot of work it was. If I never have to build another papier-mâché horse, that's fine with me!

We shook things up in 2005 with floral arrangements in bright colors like lime green and hot pink for the theme

"All Things Bright and Beautiful." Mrs. Bush suggested the color palette, which was edgier than we'd ever tried before. Over the years, the best response we got was to colors and decorations that were very traditional, so my initial reaction was that this didn't sound like Christmas. Mrs. Bush asked us to use fresh flowers everywhere, and she wanted the garlands and wreaths throughout the house to be made of fresh boxwood. Well, boxwood dries up very quickly and gets crispy, so we had to change it every week. When Mrs. Bush came down to the State Dining Room and saw us changing the garland and wreaths for the first time, she realized how extensive the upkeep was going to be. She looked at me apologetically and said, "Oh Nancy, I'm so sorry!" I'd have to say that this theme wasn't our most well received. Some of my friends loved it (mainly my designer friends who enjoy things that push the envelope), but Mrs. Bush mentioned to me that some of her friends who saw the decorations preferred the themes from previous years.

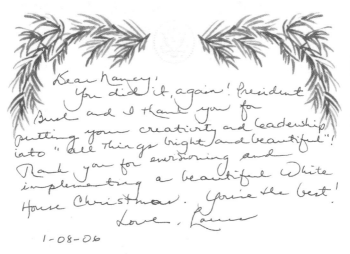

A note Mrs. Laura Bush sent me after our "All Things Bright and Beautiful" Christmas, January 8, 2006.

Here I'm putting the finishing touches on a centerpiece for the first state dinner held by President George W. Bush and the first lady, which honored President Vicente Fox of Mexico on September 5, 2001. Mrs. Bush wanted everything to be just right; in fact, to give the decorations a trial run, she and I sat down at the table as if we were guests before the actual dinner.

Mrs. Bush lights the candles in the final moments before the state dinner for President Fox begins. She's wearing a fuchsia dress, even though President Bush suggested she wear black. We included limes in the floral centerpieces in recognition of one of Mexico's major exports.

A holiday wreath hangs in a window in the Blue Room, the location of the White House's official Christmas tree. Whatever we devised as the theme for the Blue Room tree was carried over into every other room.

For the Christmas 2003 theme of children's literature, we included a figure of Harry Potter holding Hedwig the owl in front of Hogwarts Castle on the East Room mantel. I painted Harry's face, and my staff and I built the castle based on a photograph I found online.

This is the bold look that I encouraged Mrs. Laura Bush to try for the table decorations for the Governors' Dinner, February 2004. "Oh, just do it!" I told her.

Mrs. Bush and I share a moment at the press preview of the decorations for Christmas on December 2, 2004. The framed artwork is the White House Christmas card, featuring the traditional cranberry tree in the Red Room.

When we designed for outdoors, we had to be careful about what flowers we used due to the heat. We also tried to keep it simple because we were creating centerpieces for as many as 150 tables, as was the case for the congressional picnic on June 15, 2005.

For a dinner honoring Prime Minister Singh and Mrs. Kaur of India in July 2005, we created elephant centerpieces for alternating tables using green button pom-pom chrysanthemums. This was Mrs. Laura Bush's favorite centerpiece — and she even asked me to be sure to include it in this book.

Mrs. Bush at the press preview for the dinner in the State Dining Room honoring Prime Minister Junichiro Koizumi of Japan in June 2006. As centerpieces, large pavé balls of bright green cymbidium orchids float atop clear glass cylinders of alternating heights.

All the first ladies loved tulips. For First Lady Laura Bush, we created this floral arrangement of red tulips and red ilex berries, which was displayed in the Red Room in December 2006.

First Lady Laura Bush greets the press in the State Dining Room to show them the final preparations for the queen of England's visit in May 2007. Also present are staff members (from left to right) Social Secretary Amy Zantzinger, Chief Usher Steve Rochon, Pastry Chef Bill Yosses, me, and Executive Chef Cris Comerford.

Here I am — tired but nevertheless excited — meeting Queen Elizabeth II in May 2007 (and trying to hide the fact I'm wearing pants!). I was surprised by how petite the queen is.

President George W. Bush shares a toast with Queen Elizabeth II, on May 7, 2007.

President George W. Bush and First Lady Laura Bush are in the State Dining Room, just before welcoming Queen Elizabeth II and Prince Philip on May 7, 2007. The president didn't usually like wearing white tie, but White House occasions don't get more formal than this!

Mrs. Bush decides on a new china pattern with the help of Amy Zantzinger, her social secretary, and Anita McBride, her chief of staff. The pattern arrived a few weeks before President Bush left office.

We decorated tables on the Truman Balcony, which offers gorgeous views of the Washington Monument and the Jefferson Memorial, for Mrs. Laura Bush's luncheon for her staff in July 2007.

For a dinner honoring President Nicolas Sarkozy of France in November 2007, we created a dramatic look with deep orange roses and bold orange silk tablecloths.

5 Nancy Clarke
With best wishes,

President Bush sent me this inscribed photo after he visited the volunteers decorating the White House for Christmas in November 2007.

The dining table in the Red Room is set for a baseball dinner with red tulips in silver containers, the Reagan china, and linen placemats on January 22, 2008.

Our flower shop is filled with roses to be used as decorations for a dinner in the East Room honoring Pope Benedict XVI. Though the pope wasn't able to attend the dinner, he did visit the White House earlier in the day for his 81st birthday celebration on April 16, 2008.

One of the topiary centerpieces in the tent for Jenna Bush's wedding reception, held at the Bush family's Prairie Chapel Ranch in Crawford, Texas on May 10, 2008. We turned hatboxes of alternating sizes into containers for the floral arrangements.

Jenna Bush exchanges vows with Henry Hager at their wedding ceremony on May 10, 2008.

Here Mrs. Bush and I are at our last Christmas press preview together in December 2008. As she mentioned how great it was to work together, we both became misty-eyed.

My first meeting with First Lady Michelle Obama was in the East Room on January 22, 2009. Behind us from left to right are Jesse Bailey, Worthington White, and my assistant Bob Scanlan. I was grateful for the warmth of Mrs. Obama's greeting as she took my hand and said, "The flowers on the second floor are so beautiful."

President Obama surveys the flower shop refrigerator in January 2009. Soon after moving into the White House, he commented, "My favorite thing about living in the White House is the flowers."

I wanted the decorations to be perfect for President and Mrs. Obama's first formal dinner in the State Dining Room in February 2009.

Here is the last arrangement I made for the Blue Room, in May 2009, as seen on this book's cover — white lilies, green viburnum, white peonies, and white roses.

Mrs. Obama admires my granddaughter, Grace, during my retirement party in the Old Family Dining Room on May 28, 2009, with my daughter, Suzanne, my son-in-law, John, and my husband, Michael, also in attendance. The Residence staff and my staff came to see me, and former Chief Usher Gary Walters made a special trip to be there.

*To Nancy,*
*Thank you for your dedication to the White House. Good luck!*
*Michelle Obama*

A photo (signed by the first lady) taken at my retirement party, with my son-in-law, John, my husband, Michael, Mrs. Obama, me, and my daughter, Suzanne, holding my granddaughter, Grace, on May 28, 2009. Though I was glad to be surrounded by my own family, it was hard saying good-bye to my "second family."

Because of the mixed reviews on the hot pink and lime green decorations, Mrs. Bush wanted to return to a more traditional Christmas feel for 2006. She wanted to use reds and greens with red ribbons and red tablecloths and little trees decorated with snow for centerpieces. When the decorations were in place, everyone from the Residence staff to guests and even my own designers told me they felt as though Christmas looked like Christmas again.

I wasn't surprised when Mrs. Bush called to talk to me about Christmas in early January 2007. She liked to plan ahead and have all her ducks in a row. (In fact, even though she was calling to talk about Christmas 2007, she was also already thinking about holiday themes for 2008.) Every summer, Mrs. Bush and some of her friends went hiking in one of the national parks, and a close friend, Mary Bomar, who was the director of the National Park Service, came to lunch with her often. So the theme Mrs. Bush selected for Christmas 2007 was the national parks. She told me in January that she wanted canvases for oil paintings to fill each of the two nineteen-foot curved niches on the state floor. I knew it would be a construction nightmare, which it was. The staff of every shop (from the carpenters and plumbers to the engineers) jumped in to help, and we made two beautiful gold-framed curved canvases for an artist to work on. When Ken was visiting, we searched through picture books of the national parks until we found two suitable images for the artist to paint. Ken had an artist friend in Pennsylvania, Adrian Martinez, who had done a huge, beautifully detailed painting of a cow that hung on the third floor, so Mrs. Bush was very familiar with his work. He painted stunning scenes of the Grand Canyon and Zion National Park on those niche canvases, and during the holiday season, many White House guests stood in front of these enormous paintings and had their photos taken, which made me feel like the effort to construct the canvases was well worth it.

When we spoke in early 2007, Mrs. Bush had briefly mentioned red, white, and blue as a possible theme for Christmas 2008. This would be the Bushes' last Christmas in the White House, and although no one knew it yet, it was going to be my last Christmas, too, because I had decided to retire in the spring after the next administration was settled in. I wanted to start spending as much time as possible with my family, and it felt to me like the right time to go.

For Christmas 2008, Mrs. Bush wanted to feature some favorite decorations from years past, and to respond to requests that she had received over the years to use red, white, and blue as the color scheme. She wanted it to be beautiful and quite patriotic, which was tough, because most red, white, and blue decorations look more like the Fourth of July than Christmas. But we did find red stars, with a blue center, trimmed with white overlay that we could use. We ordered small silver-painted eagles with glittery wings and mixed them with silver stars in a bed of green garland with white lights. The overall effect was surprisingly Christmasy.

Every Christmas Mrs. Bush, the executive chef, the pastry chef, and I were available to the press for the press preview, and I was filled with mixed emotions during the 2008 preview — happy that we were celebrating another Christmas but sad that this one would be the last for the Bush family in the White House. Mrs. Bush wore an elegant red wool Oscar de la Renta suit, and she was very composed throughout all the questions from the press — until she introduced me. She walked over and put her arm through mine and told everyone how great it had been to work together all these years and that we had become close friends. She said, "I just want to tell you one other thing about Nancy Clarke. When we first came here in — this is going to make me weep and make her weep, too — when we first came here in January 1989 with President Bush, George's dad, the little girls, little Barbara and Jenna, who were seven, watched the parade from this inaugural parade stand that you see being built out in front of the White House now. And then they watched, they said, [the] 102 different groups that walked through. And then they came inside, and Nancy was the one that met them at the door, and she took them to the flower shop and let them make a little bouquet for their rooms. And they'll never forget it, and it was such a really sweet way for little seven-year-olds to be introduced to the White House. So thank you so much for that, Nancy. I appreciate it very much. We've had a great time working together for all these years."

We both had to fight to hold back the tears.

## Jenna's Texas Wedding

In August 2007, President and Mrs. Bush announced that Jenna was engaged to Henry Hager, and for the next several months the press and public — and the entire White House staff — wondered about the details. Would there be another White House wedding? Gossip flew everywhere. The White House social secretary, Amy Zantzinger, had heard nothing about a date or location or who would be invited. The White House chefs wondered if they would need to plan a menu. And, of course, I wondered how big the wedding would be and what kind of flowers and bouquets they would need.

But the details were completely hush-hush. Even the butlers who worked on the second floor in the Bushes' private residence had heard nothing at all. Finally, just after Christmas, little details started to leak out and we learned that Jenna had decided not to be married in the White House. She and her family wanted a very private, relaxed family wedding, and few details about the event would be disclosed. But we did learn that the wedding would take place at the Bush ranch in Crawford, Texas, on May 10, 2008. And that was that, as far as the White House staff was concerned. We wouldn't be involved with the wedding after all.

In mid-January, Mrs. Bush called me at the White House flower shop to ask if I had any fabric samples in a pale turquoise color similar to something we'd used as a tablecloth for a recent dinner in the Yellow Oval Room. It was a lovely pastel shade that the guests and even the butlers working the dinner had commented on to Mrs. Bush. With no idea that this was wedding-related, I requested five or six samples in that color range, and sent them to her as soon as they arrived.

A few days later a large envelope came to me through interoffice mail; in the envelope were the tablecloth samples and a note from Mrs. Bush on one of them that said, "This one." She didn't give me any other information. I wasn't sure if this was going to be used for an upcoming state dinner or some other event that was not yet on my radar. I figured I'd find out when Mrs. Bush was ready to tell me, but I couldn't help being curious about this intriguingly short message.

A week or so later, Mrs. Bush called again and asked if I could come upstairs to see her. And this time, she wanted to talk specifically about wedding plans. Uncertain what the extent of my involvement would be, but more than happy to help the family I'd become so close to over the years, I was delighted that she wanted my input. I assumed I would be packing all the flowers and decorations and shipping them off to Texas as we had done many times before when they held events (like personal visits with heads of state) at the ranch.

Mrs. Bush and Jenna had already done quite a bit of wedding planning by then. Jenna had selected a beautiful lake on the ranch as the site for the ceremony and chosen a local caterer and bakery to work with. They had decided that the dinner and dancing would take place outside, with dinner in one tent and dancing in a separate tent. We talked about decorating the dinner tent with large spheres of paper flowers, which is a very southwestern look, and incorporating other Texas-inspired decorations. We also discussed using giant hydrangeas, which grew on the ranch, and coordinating roses for the outdoor altar; linen choices (it turned out the pale turquoise tablecloths were indeed for Jenna's wedding); centerpieces that would complement the linens; and many other details.

In the weeks leading up to the wedding, Mrs. Bush called me every few days at 7 a.m. to go over particulars. The phone in the flower shop would ring almost as soon as I walked in the door, and the caller ID would say "Beauty Salon," so I always knew it was Mrs. Bush calling as she was getting ready for her morning.

As I've mentioned, Mrs. Bush was incredibly meticulous, so it didn't surprise me that she was giving so much attention to the tiny details of her daughter's wedding. Jenna made the big-picture decisions according to her vision, but it was her mother who made sure all the little things were exactly right.

During the course of wedding planning, I met with Mrs. Bush (and often her interior decorator, Ken Blasingame, as well as my assistant, Bob Scanlan, an excellent designer and habitual jokester) more regularly than I saw the bride-to-be — but I very much enjoyed working with Jenna when I did see her. She was twenty-six at the time, and though she used to have a reputation as a handful (she was caught drinking when she was underage), I think she was just being a typical teenager. She matured into a warm, wonderful young woman. She is friendly, outgoing, and bubbly, with great taste in clothes. At the White House, she wore beautifully tailored slacks and sweaters like her mother did, but hers always had a little youthful flair (like bell sleeves on a cashmere sweater), and she mixed high and low — an expensive sweater, for example, with trendy pants. She and her mother are very close, and they share many inside jokes — during wedding planning sessions they made each other giggle a lot. They wrote a book together that came out just a few weeks before Jenna's wedding, so they were busy promoting the book, but I did have the opportunity to work with them together a few times.

When Jenna was at the White House to talk about wedding plans, she usually sat cross-legged on the sofa, going through her notebooks of images and ideas, laughing and talking animatedly, and showing me pictures she liked from wedding magazines. I remember her being especially excited about a centerpiece she found in a magazine that was made from a hollowed-out white birch trunk. It was perfect for the rustic, naturally elegant look she was hoping to create, and she asked if we could do something like that. Someone from my staff found white birch hatboxes at a gift show in Atlanta, and we adapted them to work as containers for a liner that dropped inside. Jenna also asked me how we could incorporate serapes, the colorful patterned blankets she brought back from Panama (we used them as overlays on the outdoor tables), and talked about how to feature *papel picado* banners (*papel picado* is the Mexican folk art of intricately cut paper — for the wedding we hung them from the ceiling of the tent along with strings of lights) and festival staffs (similar to maypoles, with a sphere of paper flowers at the top of each pole that connected to colored ribbons, which cascaded down) as part of the wedding décor.

During one of these discussions, just a few weeks before the wedding, I asked Jenna if there was someone I could speak with in Texas to coordinate setup of all the flowers and decorations at the wedding site. Jenna looked at me, surprised, and said, "But you're going to go!" It was the first time anyone had mentioned that I (along with my assistant Bob) was actually going to Texas for the wedding.

On the Thursday before the wedding, we flew with the president to Texas on Air Force One. Earlier that morning, a military driver picked us up in a van and took us to Andrews Air Force Base, where I supervised the loading of the flowers into the plane's cargo bay. Standing there, in the cargo bay of Air Force One as the flowers came up its ramp, was thrilling. The military personnel were so precise in their actions — and, well, it was Air Force One! We were traveling with buckets of flowers in water, and many arrangements that we had already made and loaded into large Styrofoam containers. Everything needed to be transported carefully and packed tightly, because the cargo bay on Air Force One was completely jammed with flowers, and the large paper flower ball was hanging from a rolling rack anchored to a wall. The ribbons and centerpiece containers had traveled on a previous flight earlier that week with Mrs. Bush.

This was the only time I flew on Air Force One, and it was quite an experience. The cabins are beautiful, and the plane is divided into several compartments. The president has an office, a lounge, and sleeping quarters for long trips. There's also a medical office and several other areas filled with office equipment. The seats are nicer than anything I've ever seen on a commercial flight; they're plush leather and they recline completely for sleeping. Seats are arranged so that four people sit around a table for eating, playing cards, reading, or working. All I ate was a sandwich — and it was served on Air Force One china with linen napkins.

We landed in Waco, Texas, later that morning. Military personnel unloaded all the flowers into vans going to the ranch, and our van drove thirty miles to our motel in McGregor (a town seven miles away from the ranch — the site of the closest motel). The Bush ranch, called Prairie Chapel Ranch, spreads out across 1,600 acres. It's huge and isolated — the nearest town, Crawford, has only one traffic light. When we arrived at the ranch after checking into our motel, we went to the original farmhouse, where a refrigerator tractor-trailer sat at the end of the driveway. Members of the military and workers from Homestead Heritage (which Mrs. Bush referred to as "the Community"), a local organization whose constituents the Bushes hired to help them at the ranch, had already unloaded all the flowers into the refrigerator truck. I climbed into the truck to be sure the flowers had made the trip in good shape. Everything was perfect —incredibly, only one stem of one rose had broken when it shifted as the ice melted in the Styrofoam containers.

We set up shop in the original farmhouse, which had been converted into a guesthouse when the Bushes built their current main house. Because Mrs. Bush pays so much attention to every detail, it didn't surprise me that the guesthouse was beautiful and immaculate. It was decorated in classic southwestern style, with beautifully carved heavy wood furniture and wooden candlesticks. The wood and slate floors were polished to a shine. I knew doing our work could tear the house apart, which wouldn't be feasible since I knew the groom's family would be staying there on the day and night of the wedding. So I covered the floors with drop cloths and was as careful as I could be about keeping things picked up and clean. Members of the Community were on hand to help with the preparations, and we couldn't have finished the flowers and decorations without them.

We got to work early Friday morning, and I was standing in the driveway when I saw a cloud of dust coming down the road. As it came closer, I could see Mrs. Bush driving a white pickup truck. I'll never forget seeing her speeding up to the guesthouse with dust flying everywhere and her mother, Jenna Welsh, in the passenger seat. She wanted to check in to see how things were going with the flowers before a luncheon for Jenna and wedding rehearsal festivities. She climbed a ladder to get into the back of the massive refrigerator truck so she could see for herself how everything looked. And she told me that the local Texas wildflowers known as bluebells were blooming, and that Jenna hoped we could incorporate some of them into the arrangements.

As soon as she left, Bob and I worked with eight local ladies from the Community on the centerpieces and cake base. I decided that no matter how late we all had to work, we would finish all the centerpieces, cake flowers, boutonnieres, and festival staffs on Friday. That way, on Saturday all we would have to do was to make the bouquets and hair flowers and transport everything either to the Bushes' home or to the tents.

By the time we had almost completed everything, it was near dusk and we were ready for a break. The ranch foreman offered to give us a tour of the ranch, which was helpful because we still needed to find bluebells blooming in the fields. So Ken, Bob, and I headed out, riding on the gate of a pickup truck. Miles away from shelter, after we'd found the bluebells, the foreman got a call from the Secret Service. A terrible storm was moving in fast, very fast, and we needed to get back to safety. The foreman gunned the accelerator and we had a bumpy ride on the gate of the truck as it sped through the tall grass and dirt paths. We made it back to the dinner tent, where our cars were parked and where we'd been working on the paper decorations, just as the skies opened up. I have never seen it rain so hard — not to mention the hail and wind. The sides of the tent were flapping and the top was filling up with water and beginning to sag. Luckily, we hadn't placed any flower arrangements in the tent yet. "Get out!" the workers from the tent company called out to us. "You must leave the tent for your own safety." Bedraggled from the downpour, we retreated to the guesthouse without finishing putting together the paper decorations. As the wind swept through the fields and the rain continued hammering the tent long into the night, we headed back to our motel exhausted.

At dawn on Saturday morning, everything was still. Bob and I returned to the ranch before daybreak to check on the tents and the decorations and to take stock of what kind of damage had been wreaked by the storm. We entered through the adjoining kitchen tent and gazed all around. When I saw what the storm had done to the kitchen tent — hail holes punched in the canvas, portable ovens upended, crates of china and glassware filled with water — my heart sank. I was almost afraid to look at the decorations that we'd already put in place. But things were not as bad as I feared. Some streamers had loosened from the festival staffs and dangled on the ground, soaked, and some of the paper flowers were wet. We trimmed the streamers that were too drenched to salvage, fluffed up the flower sphere, and installed fans to dry everything out. Some of the *papel picado* banners had fallen to the ground while others had come unstrung. The workers from the Community rehung as many as were salvageable and replaced those that were ruined. Luckily, the storm was completely gone, and the day was going to be hot — perfect for drying things out.

While we were unloading the centerpieces from the refrigerator truck into the dinner tent to place them on the tables, former President and Barbara Bush came to say hello. "Nancy," she said as she hugged me, "do you realize that you have done the weddings for *two* President Bush's daughters?" I laughed and said, "How wonderful! I hadn't thought of that yet." She laughed too, and I got right back to work.

We returned to the guesthouse to make bouquets and headpieces for Jenna and her twin sister, Barbara, and small nosegays for the grandmothers. Jenna's bouquet featured white mini calla lilies, white floribunda, white campanula, white sweet William, white lisianthus, 'Bianca' roses, and white ranunculus. For her sister, I made a bouquet to match her pale lavender dress (by designer Lela Rose) of lavender floribunda, 'Bianca' roses, blue delphinium, white campanula, and white sweet William, and a matching flower crown. The bridesmaids weren't going to carry flowers; they wore knee-length chiffon dresses, also by Lela Rose, in an array of colors meant to evoke the wildflowers of Texas. Boutonnieres for the men and nosegays for the mothers of the bride and groom were all white.

We finished by late morning, and then we needed to move everything out of the guesthouse quickly, before the groom's family arrived. We cleaned up our mess, and Bob and Ken went off to work on the altar flower arrangements, which they made from white roses and hydrangeas grown on the ranch, while I jumped into the back of the refrigerator truck and rode the mile or so with men from the Community to the wedding tent to unload the centerpieces and place them on the tables. The centerpieces — a mix of high globe-shaped topiaries and low arrangements, placed in such a way that the view to the head table was never blocked — were made of lavender and white campanula, purple clematis, blue and green hydrangeas, white lisianthus, white roses, and camellia foliage. It was a beautiful combination of garden flowers.

The midday heat was like an oppressive furnace. I used the same flowers we'd used in the centerpieces to put the finishing touches on the wedding cake, a four-tiered, traditional Mexican *tres leches* ("three milks") cake with whipped cream frosting. Even with air conditioning running, it was so hot that the layers started to slide a bit. The ladies from the bakery assembling the layers were worried that the tiers might not stay in place, but they couldn't do anything about it at this point. I decorated the base of the cake with flowers to match the centerpieces and placed a few flowers on each tier and a small matching bouquet on the top. The president came over to pose with me for a photograph that I never show anyone, because I looked so awful. My hair was wet with sweat, my makeup smeared from the heat. I was a mess.

After we installed the centerpieces and Bob and Ken finished the altar arrangements, Bob and I got a ride to the main ranch house to deliver the wedding party's flowers. The Bushes' house is a long, single-level ranch house built from local limestone with a galvanized tin roof. It's impeccably decorated in contemporary style with a mixture of heavy wicker, wood, and wrought-iron furniture that stands out against the pale beige walls and stone of the interior. Inside, the house was a flurry of activity. Jenna and her twin sister, Barbara, as well as Laura Bush and Jenna's fourteen attendants, were running around getting ready. Some were already in their colorful dresses; others were in slips or robes. Jenna hadn't yet donned her Oscar de la Renta gown. The girls were all laughing and talking about their hair, their makeup, and how much time they had left before the ceremony.

I left their flowers for them and went to shower and clean up for the big event. Almost immediately, my Blackberry rang. It was Jenna. She asked me to come back to the house because Barbara's hairpiece was too big. A driver picked Bob and me up in a golf cart and rushed us back. We fixed the flower crown in the back of the golf cart while President and Mrs. Bush and the girls were setting up for family photos. President Bush wore a dark suit with a pastel blue tie, and Mrs. Bush looked gorgeous in her deep turquoise dress. They were all happy and excited. Just before the first photo was snapped, I placed the crown on Barbara's head, and before I slipped away, Mrs. Bush — calm as always — said to me, "Everything is beautiful."

By 5:00 p.m., when the ceremony began, the weather had cooled off enough to be comfortable. Bob and I stopped working for a few minutes and stood off to the side so we could see President Bush drive Jenna to the aisle in the same white pickup truck Mrs. Bush had been using the day before. They got out of the truck and with little fanfare he walked her down the aisle. It was a simple, lovely ceremony.

While the guests were having cocktails and eating dinner, we set up the dancing tent with colorful festival staffs, and members of the Community strung colored *papel picado* on the tent's open framework. I peeked into the dinner tent and saw President and Mrs. Bush and heard a snippet of the president's toast. He may have been the president, but his toast was a typical father-of-the-bride speech. When the dinner was finished, Bob, Ken, and I attended the dancing reception, which lasted until 4:00 in the morning, but after getting up before dawn the morning of the wedding, we only made it until midnight. The 280 guests had a wonderful time, celebrating into the wee hours.

It was a great party — a relaxed wedding with a strong Texas vibe. The overall feeling was very comfortable, and the guests were mainly family members and close friends. Jenna had grown up in Texas, and that's what she wanted. Because I had known the girls while they were children and their grandfather was president, I was so glad to be a part of this day, and so honored to have been included. Bob and I felt like we had done a White House wedding, but out of the back of a truck. The next morning, we flew back to Washington, again on Air Force One, with the President

May 20, 2008

JENNA BUSH

Dear Nancy,

Thanks so very much for all of your help, support, and love in making our wedding so very special + beautiful. It was so fun to work with you and see your creativity shape the evening! Here is a small token of my appreciation + love! I hope you like the small flower and it

will always remind you of the flowers + happiness you've brought into my life. My first experience as a little girl, when my Grampy had just been elected President, was a trip with you to make a bouquet. Now after eight years I will never forget the beautiful flowers you arranged for my wedding!

Love, Jenna + Henry

Dear Nancy,

Thank you for making Jenna's wedding one of the most beautiful weddings ever! I loved working with you on the wedding just like I've loved working with you for these seven years. You're an artist and you're wonderful to work with. With much love,

May 21, 2008      Laura Bush

(top) A note from Jenna Bush and her husband, Henry Hager, thanking me for my help with their wedding, May 20, 2008; (bottom) I received a lovely thank-you note from Mrs. Laura Bush as well, May 21, 2008.

159

and Mrs. Bush, and former President George Bush and Mrs. Barbara Bush, too. The former president came through and said hello to everyone on the plane.

The day the Bushes left the White House in 2009, the whole family came in to say good-bye to the Residence staff. Jenna cried as she hugged me, and thanked me again for helping with her wedding. I told Mrs. Bush that when Barbara gets married, Bob and I will be there to help at her wedding, too. She smiled and said we would keep in touch. And we still do.

# A New Era: Michelle Obama

*As you look back on your years of service in the White House, I hope you can see what an extraordinary career you have had. You should be so proud of everything you have accomplished. So much history and so many memories have been adorned with your work. You have brought beauty into the lives of so many presidents and their families.*

*I hope you enjoy a wonderful retirement, Nancy. You have earned it.*

*— Michelle Obama*

I n the summer of 2008, I decided that I would retire from the White House the following spring. I'd been working at the White House for thirty years, and the long days and early mornings were beginning to wear on me. I was ready to spend more time with my husband and the rest of my family — and I'd just learned that my daughter was pregnant with my first grandchild! I wanted to keep working through the end of the Bush administration (and help Laura Bush with her final Christmas) and lead my staff into the beginning of the new administration. At that point, of course, we didn't know who would be moving into 1600 Pennsylvania Avenue come January. I wanted to wait until after the new administration was in place to let the chief usher know about my decision, because I felt that the new team should be involved with choosing my successor.

I'm so glad I waited to retire, because I was around for the beginning of the Obama administration, which brought fever-pitch excitement to Washington and the country. It was such a groundbreaking election, and the Obamas seemed to be ushering a new, youthful, forward-thinking era into the White House.

What's more, being there for the Obama inaugural meant I got to spend the night at the White House for the very first time. Alas, it wasn't as glamorous as it sounds. I didn't exactly sleep in the Lincoln Bedroom, but rather on an air mattress on the floor in the curator's office. I live in Virginia, and all bridges into the city were being closed at 1:00 a.m. on Inauguration Day, so if I wanted to be at the White House that day, I needed to stay over *somewhere*. The easiest option was crashing on the floor. Still, it's fun to say I have indeed slept at the White House.

Prior to the Obamas' arrival, I met with Desirée Rogers, their confident and accomplished social secretary, to talk about a late-night "breakfast" the Obamas wanted to host after the inaugural balls. She told me they liked fairly casual entertaining and the opportunity to mingle and enjoy their guests. No other president and first lady had planned an event like this, and it sounded like fun! We decided to fill the East Room with cabaret tables decorated with arrangements of mini lavender calla lilies and roses surrounded by votive candles. The Jonas Brothers would be performing, and Oprah was on the guest list, along with seventy other friends, family members, and celebrities. On inauguration night, I left around midnight, after the party was set up but before it started. Even though I missed the festivities, I could tell that people were going to have a good time.

I helped Mrs. Obama's interior decorator, Michael Smith, set up the second floor on Inauguration Day. Though we didn't totally finish the redecoration that day, and in fact Michael and Mrs. Obama were still working on the redecoration of the Residence when I left, I did see that the furniture and style she was bringing in were more contemporary and casual than that of other administrations. Over the course of her first few months in the White House, Mrs. Obama also changed many of the older paintings for modern and abstract ones from the National Gallery of Art, including bold works by Mark Rothko and Jasper Johns, and Ed Ruscha's "I Think I'll . . . ," a large, mostly red painting featuring snippets of text such as, "Maybe . . . no . . . " and "Wait a minute . . . I . . . I." Other works Mrs. Obama selected included paintings by Native American and African American artists and the nineteenth-century artist George Caitlin. I have eclectic taste in art. I like everything from ultra-traditional to contemporary, so it was fun for me to see famous examples of modern art up close.

Michael decorated the Obama girls' rooms using furniture from stores like Pottery Barn and Anthropologie, and he installed traditional chandeliers that had been transformed into contemporary pieces by replacing their crystals with colorful circles. I kept a small vase of pink tulips in Sasha's room and purple anemones in Malia's room. Mrs. Obama chose a four-poster bed for the bedroom she shares with the president, which seemed out of character for her contemporary tastes, yet somehow fit perfectly into the room as she was decorating it with new draperies and carpet and contemporary paintings. In their bedroom, I placed a clear vase of tall flowering branches, which worked with both the traditional and contemporary elements in the room.

Given what I'd learned about Mrs. Obama's (mostly!) contemporary preferences, as we were preparing the second floor for the Obamas' first homecoming on Inauguration Day, for the West Hall I filled a tall, large, clear glass cylinder with yellow cymbidium orchids. This was a considerably more modern arrangement than I would have used for any other first lady. The container was simple, the orchids were large and sleek, and it was an eye-catching addition to the large room. She told Bob, my assistant, that she loved it.

Two days after Inauguration Day, the ushers' office asked the whole Residence staff to assemble in the East Room. We lined up in a semicircle before Mrs. Obama entered the room. She first spoke to all of us as a group about how happy she was to have such a great staff, and she told us that we (and our families) would be included as guests at many events. Then she came around and talked to everyone individually. This was my first time actually meeting her. She had her hair pulled back into a knot at the nape of her neck, and she wore a navy tank top and navy pants. I was surprised by how tall she is, even wearing flats, and I thought she was quite striking, with a beautiful face. Her clothes, in general, were younger and trendier looking than those of any other first lady, and she has brought lots of attention to up-and-coming American fashion designers by wearing their pieces.

"The flowers on the second floor are so beautiful," she said to me as she took my hand. "Thank you. And the flowers in the girls' rooms are just perfect." The president followed a few minutes behind her, wearing a dark suit. His appearance also surprised me — I couldn't believe how thin he is. Like Mrs. Obama, he spoke to the whole group first. "Thank you for making my family feel so welcome here," he said. "I want to get to know all of you and what your jobs are." Then he came around to speak to everyone one at a time. He shook my hand, and I introduced myself as the chief floral designer. He grinned and said, "My favorite thing about living in the White House is the flowers!" Of course, the comment delighted me and my whole staff. "Thank you, Mr. President," I replied. "I am so happy to hear that."

For the next few months, I worked mainly with Mrs. Obama's social secretary, Desirée Rogers, instead of directly with Mrs. Obama. (This was before the infamous incident when two uninvited individuals got into a state dinner, which Desirée took a lot of heat for; that happened after I left!) I got the impression that Mrs. Obama was much more laid-back than previous first ladies and let her staff make many event decisions for her — she was more focused on taking care of her girls and helping them adjust to living in the White House. But Desirée and I showed her a sample for her very first formal dinner, the February Governors' Dinner. She was quite easygoing about it. She chose a pale green linen tablecloth, pedestals and wine coolers from the vermeil collection for flower containers, and a flower arrangement of purple and red tulips, red roses, purple calla lilies, and red Mokara orchids. At Desirée's urging, Mrs. Obama also made an unusual china choice, opting to use base plates from the 1939 World's Fair china, which we alternated with the base plates Mrs. Eisenhower had purchased to complement the Truman china. Her dress for that dinner was black and strapless, and she wore it with many strings of pearls in different lengths. She looked stunningly beautiful.

The ushers' office let me know that both President and

Mrs. Obama wanted bowls of Gala apples in their offices in lieu of flower arrangements. We ended up having to check and replenish those bowls every day, because staff and guests kept eating the apples. In the Residence, Mrs. Obama preferred clean, simple arrangements — she especially loved calla lilies. She also asked me if we could label the varieties in flower arrangements (which we did with small signs the calligraphers made) to help her and the girls sort out the names of different flowers. Occasionally, the girls colored on the signs, but I hope they learned from them,

THE WHITE HOUSE

February 4, 2009

Ms. Nancy Clarke

Dear Nancy,

Thank you so much for the warm and welcoming birthday reception. The cake and book were very thoughtful gestures and made for a wonderful welcome to the White House. I look forward to working with you and getting to know you and your family over the next four years.

All the best,

*Michelle Obama*

Michelle Obama

Mrs. Obama sent me this appreciative note for my help on her birthday reception, February 4, 2009.

too — I thought it was a great idea. Whenever I saw them, the girls were very sweet and polite. The housekeeper told me she was not allowed to make their beds — they had to make their own beds and clean their own rooms. As a mother of two children, I thought that was a great policy, even if they were living at the White House. Mrs. Obama's mother, Marian Robinson, who lived in the White House with the Obamas so she could help take care of the girls, was incredibly gracious. I've rarely felt that my work has been as appreciated by anyone; Mrs. Robinson never wanted us to remove flower arrangements, even when they were almost totally wilted, because, she said, "They're just so pretty and I hate to see them go!"

## Time to Go

In March 2009, I finally let the chief usher know about my decision to retire, and then I had to tell my staff, which I dreaded. When I returned to the shop after my routine walk-through on a Monday morning, I quickly announced, "I have decided to retire at the end of May." It was a bit abrupt, but I wanted to get it out on the table immediately — and it was difficult for me even to bring it up. Although I'd dropped several hints in prior months, they were shocked, and they worried about who would take my place. They'd thought I'd always be there. Keith, one of my designers, told me he expected I would be a 90-year-old lady making centerpieces.

I wanted to let Mrs. Obama know, too, as soon as possible. And I wanted to tell her myself. So when I saw her in the hall, on her way to her East Wing office, I said, "Mrs. Obama, if you have a minute, I'd like to talk to you." She stopped and I said, "I'm going to be retiring in May." She looked concerned and asked, "Is anything wrong?"

"Oh, no," I replied. "My husband is going to be 71, and my daughter is having our first grandbaby, and I want to spend more time with my family. I think it's a good time for me to go and for you to select a new florist." As I was talking to her, I started to cry, and she hugged me and said, "You will always be welcome in the White House."

Leaving my job was bittersweet for me. I hated to leave my staff. I'd been with them for years, and they had become close friends — not to mention a supremely talented group of designers. (In fact, it took seven months for the White House to hire my replacement, and my staff handled everything beautifully on their own during that time.) I loved seeing them every day and getting to know their personalities, and I especially loved the sense of pride, teamwork, and accomplishment we had every time we worked on an event together. But I was also ready to leave. I was looking forward to sleeping in past 4:20 in the morning, and having more time with my family. I had missed so many recitals and school plays and PTA meetings while my kids were growing up, and I had to cut our family vacations short several times so I could get back to the White House. I was ready to be there for my family full-time.

I was also looking forward to arranging flowers in my own home and in my own taste for a change. While working at the White House, I rarely had the time or energy for that. At Christmas especially, I just had no interest. One year, our tree at home had no ornaments on it until someone gave me one at work and I came home that night and threw it on our tree. Another year, I was so tired of Christmas decorating that I wasn't even going to get a tree, but my husband and children threw a fit. They wouldn't dare pick one without my supervision, so one night on my way home from work, I pulled into a tree lot, popped open my trunk, and asked the man to throw any tree in my trunk. "I don't care what it looks like," I said. I was just too tired to get out of the car. When I got it home, my husband set it up — and it turned out to be one of the prettiest trees we ever had.

These days I don't do any formal arrangements — I just put water in a vase and throw in a bunch of my favorite flowers. Like Mrs. Reagan, I adore peonies (I have ever since I was little, when my grandparents had them growing in their yard), and I buy them when they are in season and don't cost a fortune. I like lily of the valley, viburnum, blue and white hydrangeas, bright floribunda roses, and rich summer-colored asters — pretty much anything that smells great and looks pretty. Unlike certain former first ladies I know, I'm not too picky.

Two days before my last day, the ushers' office hosted a going-away reception for me in the Old Family Dining Room on the state floor. The whole Residence staff attended, and so did Mrs. Obama (who spent a lot of time talking to my daughter and her newborn baby; I love the photo I have of them together). Gary Walters, the former chief usher, also attended, and I was so happy to see him and to know that he was, in fact, surviving — and thriving — in retirement.

The current chief usher, Admiral Rochon, presented me with a plaque of large gold coins in a beautiful frame, one coin to represent each of the six presidents that I had served. I started to cry and my staff was also crying, so when it was my turn to speak, I almost couldn't do it. I choked back tears long enough to say, "Thank you all for becoming my second family. I will miss you." These people really had become my family as well as my friends, and I knew I would miss each and every one terribly. Before the party ended, Mrs. Obama said to me, "We are so sorry to lose you, but we understand . . . and we hope to see you at Christmas." (The idea of going back at Christmastime sounds like fun, but I don't think it would be fair to the current chief floral designer if I showed up — so I don't think I ever will.)

My last day came on Friday, May 30, and I was a mess. I turned in my White House pass at the ushers' office, which made everything seem so final. A pass is something that everyone who works at the White House wears proudly, and now mine was gone. I cried all the way to my car and all the way home, and then I cried for most of the weekend. I had left a place that meant so much to me, where I'd become friends not only with the other staff members, but with some absolutely incredible first ladies. How could I ever forget the moments I shared with my first ladies? My first Christmas in the White House, seeing Mrs. Carter for the first time as she came down the hall to thank all the volunteers, or laughing with Mrs. Reagan when she asked (for the umpteenth time) for peonies out of season, or catching the twinkle in Mrs. Barbara Bush's eye as she stood in her Keds and helped me hang needlepoint ornaments on the stately Noble fir in the Blue Room, or watching Mrs. Clinton clap with excitement at the beauty of the tables majestically set for a state dinner, or standing with Mrs. Laura Bush, both of us holding back tears at our last Christmas together in the White House, or listening to Mrs. Obama's gracious words and shaking her hand as she thanked me for thirty years of service at my farewell reception. I'm forever grateful that I had the opportunity to serve them. I truly believe I had the ultimate job any floral designer could ever dream of, and at the end of a long career, that's a very satisfying feeling.

THE WHITE HOUSE

May 22, 2009

Nancy K. Clarke

Dear Nancy:

I wanted to take a moment to congratulate you on your retirement. As you look back on your years of service in the White House, I hope you can see what an extraordinary career you have had.

You should be so proud of everything you have accomplished. So much history and so many memories have been adorned with your work, and you have brought beauty into the lives of so many Presidents and their families.

And although these last few months have gone so quickly, I wanted to thank you for all of your hard work and everything you have done to make my family and me feel at home as we have settled in here at the White House.

I hope you enjoy a wonderful retirement, Nancy. You have earned it.

Sincerely,

Michelle Obama

A letter Mrs. Obama sent me when I retired, May 22, 2009.

# Appendix

The following keepsakes are special items that bring back happy memories of my twenty-five years as the chief floral designer at the White House.

## Dinner
*Honoring*
His Excellency
The General Secretary of the Central Committee
of the Communist Party of the Soviet Union
and Mrs. Gorbachev

Columbia River Salmon &
Lobster Medallions en Gelée
Caviar Sauce
Fennel Seed Twists

Loin of Veal with Wild Mushrooms
Champagne Sauce
Tarragon Tomatoes
Corn Turban

Medley of Garden Greens
Brie Cheese with Crushed Walnuts
Vinegar & Avocado Oil Dressing

Tea Sorbet in Honey Ice Cream

JORDAN Chardonnay 1984
STAGS' LEAP Cabernet Sauvignon Lot 2 1978
IRON HORSE Brut Summit Cuvée 1984

### THE WHITE HOUSE
Tuesday, December 8, 1987

The state dinner menu in honor of the General Secretary of the USSR Mikhail Gorbachev and Mrs. Gorbachev, December 8, 1987.

## White House Millennium Dinner

A Taste of
Beluga Caviar, Lobster, Foie Gras,
Oyster Velouté
Sterling Chardonnay "Winery Lake" 1998

Truffle-Marinated Rack of Lamb
Roasted Artichoke and Pepper Ragout
Crispy Garlic Polenta
Dehlinger Pinot Noir "Reserve" 1997

Salad of Winter Greens
with Golden and Red Beets
Blue Cheese Tartine

A New Millennium Celebration
Chocolate and Champagne Delight
Iron Horse Brut "Millennium Cuvée"

It is our distinct honor to welcome you to the White House for a Millennium Salute to American Achievement. Pen to paper, brush to canvas, hands to clay, idea to reality—Americans have demonstrated our endless capacity to express the freedom and creativity that our democracy has nurtured over the last two centuries. On the eve of a new millennium, we continue to influence, ever responding, democracy around the world, a global marketplace of ideas, and human achievements inevitable journey toward peace and justice. America's song of freedom and ingenuity—our great gift to the twentieth century—thrives within our unique symphony of races and cultures. Because of the determination and innovation of two centuries of indomitable Americans—pioneers, everyone, are emboldened as never before to question, challenge and create. Tonight we pledge to honor our past and imagine our future by working together to foster creativity and freedom of thought, welfare for others into the realms of possibility, and achieve justice and equality. Tonight, as we celebrate all that is great about America, all that is intrinsic to the American spirit, we welcome the dawn of our future.

William Clinton            Hillary Rodham Clinton

The White House Millennium Dinner menu, December 31, 1999.

## CHELSEA CLINTON

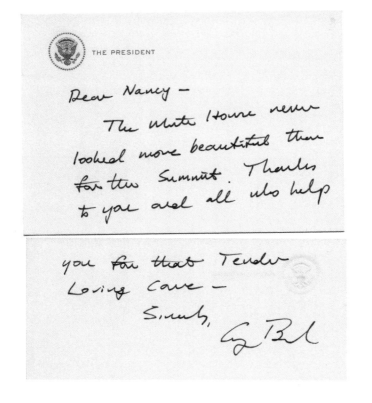

Dear Nancy,

Thank you for spending so much time with my friends and me. All of that time was filled with joy. Everything the flowers, you, your staff and your love of what you create, created that joy. Thank you again –

Chelsea

(top) A thank you note from Chelsea Clinton after I taught her and her friends basic flower design; (bottom) A note from President George H.W. Bush thanking me for the flowers for his historic summit meeting with Soviet President Mikhail Gorbachev that began on May 31, 1990.

THE PRESIDENT

Dear Nancy –

The White House never looked more beautiful than for this Summit. Thanks to you and all who help you for that Tender Loving Care –

Sincerely,

G Bush

### Flower Shop Questions for Mrs. Bush

**General questions**

- Are you or the President or any members of your family allergic to any flowers? —NO

- Do you or the President have favorite flowers or favorite colors of flowers? *I like roses & lilies - also zennias & other summer annuals*
- Are there any flowers or colors of flowers that you would prefer we do not use?

- Do you prefer a certain style of flower arrangement to another style, e.g., formal, casual, traditional, contemporary, loose, tight, tall, short, combinations, etc.? *I like a variety of style of arrangements*
- Do you like object d'art mixed with flowers for centerpieces? *no*

- Do you like vases of flowering branches when they are in season? *yes*

- Do you like greenery mixed in with the flowers or flowers only? *Usually flowers only - unless the greenery does not look like filler.*
- Do you like flower arrangements in clear vases where the stems are visible? *OK*

- Once a day we check the 2nd and 3rd floor flowers, generally, when would it be convenient for my staff or me to check the flowers? Weekends? *8:30 or so*

**2nd Floor dinners**

- What type of flower arrangements would you like to use for 2nd Floor private dinners or family dinners?

- Would you object to a series of small glass vases or bud vases filled with flowers for a centerpiece on a rectangular table? *no*

- What type of candlesticks do you prefer? *Silver & vermeil*

- We have found it necessary to use a type of taper candle which is an off-white metal cylinder filled with a small wax candle insert as the air conditioning system causes the wax to spatter if we use regular candles. Is it okay to continue to use these candles? *yes*

- Do you like votive candles? *yes*

- Do you like place mats on the natural wood or tablecloths? *both*

- Do you object to mixing silver and vermeil on the same table? All of our china *no* patterns are gold-banded, however we gave both silver flatware and vermeil flatware available. We also have silver and gold candlesticks.

- Do you prefer to use one china pattern for 2nd Floor dinners exclusively or would you prefer we select different patterns based on the particular dinner and flowers available? *different patterns*

**Formal Dinners**

- When we have heads-of-state staying at Blair House for State Dinners, the President and First Lady have traditionally sent flowers when they arrive, (a crystal bowl of roses) would you like to continue this practice? If so, do you wish to send a personal card or should we use your engraved cards?

- Do you wish to coordinate your dress with the flowers and tablecloths?

- Is there any type of tablecloth or color of tablecloth you especially like to use for formal dinners?

- Traditionally, I have prepared sample flower arrangements and complete table settings for the First Lady and her Social Secretary to review. Do you wish to discuss some of the options prior to my making the samples or should I coordinate with Cathy, and then prepare samples for you and Cathy?

A general questionnaire given to first ladies when they first arrive at the White House. This one is addressed to Mrs. Laura Bush.

THE WHITE HOUSE

January 7, 2003

Mrs. Nancy Clarke

Dear Nancy,

Another masterpiece! *All Creatures Great and Small* brought countless smiles to faces throughout the White House this holiday season. President Bush and I are enormously grateful to you for the splendid execution of a delightful theme.

Our White House elves reported having spotted you up to your elbows in papier maché in the flower shop, putting the finishing touches on a handsome dog, while at the very same moment you were seen on a ladder in the East Colonnade adding just a few more red berries to a lovely wreath and in the Blue Room supervising the placement of yet another cardinal on the tree!

Thank you for your months of careful planning and preparation and weeks of concentrated effort and direction which produced such a marvelous result.

The President and I hope that 2003 is beginning with some well-earned relaxation for you!

With gratitude and admiration,

*Laura Bush*

A letter from Mrs. Laura Bush thanking me for the Christmas decorations for "All Creatures Great and Small," January 7, 2003.

Jenna likes this color for table cloth. We would need 26 at least - 25 tables for meals - 1 for cake -

07, 2008 8:26 AM
sey M.
y

t@fwmsh.org>

Nancy - This is a large flower farm in Texas that we used to use when the Prez was Gov. We could have someone pick these up to

Jenna, here is some information from the flower farm your mom referenced. Please let me know if you'd like me to follow up with any additional questions to them.

Sounds pretty.

----------------

From: Frank and Pamela Arnosky
Sent: Sun 1/6/2008 8:18 PM
To: Clare Pritchett
Subject: Re: flowers in may

for altar purple, orange to white roses

Hello Clare,
There are beautiful flowers in May--snapdragons and delphiniums...some of the wildflowers such as coreopsis, cornflowers, achillea, queen anne's lace. There should be some campanula, lilies, and tall dianthus, also. I am thinking back, rather than referring to last year's sales figures at this moment. This date in May is too early for the sunflowers or zinnias to be blooming.
Is the wedding to be in the Austin area? Would you be coming to the farm to pick them up?
Hope this helps, and look forward to hearing from you later on, if you all will be planning on getting the flowers from us.
Best wishes,
Pamela Arnosky
Arnosky Family Farms

Texas Specialty Cut Flowers
www.texascolor.com

Lots of white, green: blue/purple

+ other flowers from regular florist

On Jan 6, 2008, at 1:18 PM, Clare Pritchett wrote:

Can you share what flowers you will be growing in May? I am working on a May 10 wedding and would like to know options available.

An email with Mrs. Laura Bush's notations about Jenna's upcoming wedding.

**THE WHITE HOUSE**

WASHINGTON

January 14, 2009

Mrs. Nancy Clarke

Dear Nancy,

Thank you for your outstanding service to America's first families –
and for your devotion and friendship to ours.  You have given so
generously of your time and talent to make the White House a home
for us and a welcoming place for our guests and friends.

We are especially grateful to you for your splendid floral
arrangements that brighten the White House and delight all who see
them.  And what marvelous additions you have made to the
holidays!  Each year you and your staff have done a simply amazing
job of bringing our ideas to life with your imagination and
creativity.

We will always have fond memories of our time in the White House
and appreciate your dedication and hard work.  Best wishes to you
and your family.

With warm regards,

A note from President George W. Bush and Mrs. Laura Bush thanking me for being
with them at the White House, January 14, 2009.

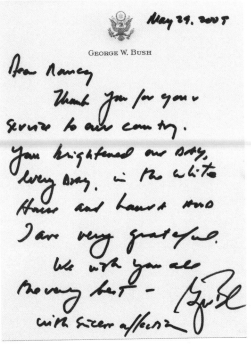

(top) A note from President George W. Bush on my retirement, May 29, 2009;
(bottom) A note from Mrs. Barbara Bush thanking me for my years of service to the
White House, April 3, 2009.

OFFICE OF NANCY REAGAN

April 29, 2009

Dear Nancy,

I heard about your upcoming retirement, and even though
I understand your reasons, I can't help but be a little sorry to hear
the news. I don't know if the White House will ever be the same
without you.

I often look back on our years in the White House and remember
fondly your wonderful creations. From elaborate state dinners to
informal arrangements for the Residence, your artistry was
always evident.

You have every reason to be proud of thirty years of service to
six Presidents, their families and their guests. I know that for all
those years you sacrificed time with your family and missed
many personal special events in order to accommodate the
schedule of the President and the White House. Now that you
are beginning a new chapter in your life, I wish you all the
happiness that you deserve.

Warmly,

*Nancy Reagan*

Ms. Nancy Clarke
Usher's Office/The Residence
The White House
Washington, District of Columbia 20500

A letter from Mrs. Reagan, sending me good wishes for my retirement.

# ACKNOWLEDGMENTS

I would like to thank:

Christie Matheson, for helping me to turn my thoughts into words.

Jane Dystel, for helping me to find the right publisher.

Megan Hiller, Mark Chimsky-Lustig, and the rest of the team at Sellers Publishing, for making this book a reality.

Gary Walters, the former White House Chief Usher, for being a dear friend and mentor, and for reminding me of details that had faded from my memory.

Ronn Payne, Wendy Elsasser, Keith Fulghum, Bob Scanlan, and Jesse Bailey, for always having my back; for being my family away from home for so many years; and for filling in the fine details as I worked on this book.

The White House Curators for digging up historical particulars and helping me to be sure that the information in the book is accurate.

The White House Historical Association for providing beautiful high-resolution photographs, and information to go with each photo.

The Jimmy Carter Library, the Ronald Reagan Library, the George H. W. Bush Library, the William J. Clinton Library, the George W. Bush Library, and the White House Photo Office, for providing photos — and directions on how to use them properly.

The White House Ushers' Office, for giving me support over the years — and correct sequences and technical terms for this book.

And a very special thank you to my family, my friends, and my research assistant, for helping me sort through thirty years of memorabilia and recall so many details. My endless appreciation goes to all of you.

# INDEX